The Essential Career Guide for the Scientific Professional

Barbara Gebhardt

The Essential Career Guide for the Scientific Professional

Barbara Gebhardt

in cooperation with

DataMotion Publishing, LLC

New York

The Essential Career Guide for the Scientific Professional

Library of Congress Control Number: 2012935707

ISBN: 978-0-9815831-8-1

DataMotion Publishing, LLC
1019 Fort Salonga Road, Suite 10-333
Northport, NY 11768-2209
www.datamotionpublishing.com

Table of Contents

About the Author 3

Warning–Disclaimer 7

Introduction...9

~~~~~~~~~~

Chapter 1: Occupational Opportunities in
the Scientific Field 11

Chapter 2: Transitioning from Academia to
Industry..75

Chapter 3: Resumes 81

Chapter 4: Interviewing Basics 95

Chapter 5: Excelling at the Job Interview 105

Chapter 6: Working With a Search Firm.........123

Chapter 7: Networking.......................................129

Chapter 8: Developing Your Elevator Pitch ...135

Chapter 9: Career and Job Fairs......................139

Chapter 10: Contract and Temporary
Employment 143

Chapter 11: Social Media and Social
Networking 149

Chapter 12: Tips From a Recruiter 159

Chapter 13: Associations and Professional
Groups 163

Chapter 14: Journals, Publications and
Additional Resources 219

Coming Soon 249

About DataMotion Publishing 251

About the Author

Barbara Gebhardt

Barbara Gebhardt has been in the employment field since 1981. Starting her career with Career Blazers, she went on to open its first franchise in 1987. She later opened a Career Blazers training center which successfully integrated training and placement and became the model for sites nationwide. The training center on Long Island focused on the training and subsequent placement of workers displaced due to corporate downsizing on Long Island.

In 1996, Gebhardt became Executive Vice President / Chief Operating Officer of Career Blazers, responsible for all company operations while continuing to operate the office on Long Island. After the completion of five years in the role and achievement of a series of corporate objectives, Gebhardt was again dedicating herself to staffing on Long Island. In June of 2004, Gebhardt created Opus Staffing and separated from the Career Blazers franchise program.

In 2006, she added a new division, Opus Scientific, to keep locally trained scientists on Long Island and attract scientific talent to the area. Opus Scientific provides temporary and contract staffing, contract to hire and direct hire staffing to the biotechnology, pharmaceutical, medical device, cosmetic, chemical, environmental and other scientific intensive industries that require skilled talent. This division quickly expanded nationally.

Gebhardt serves on the Regional Board of the American Heart Association. She serves on the Stony Brook University Corporate Education and Training Advisory Board and the Advisory Board of the Advanced Energy Research and Technology Center. She is on the Board of the New York Biotechnology Association and develops human resources, leadership and clean technology tracks for its Annual Conference. Gebhardt currently serves as Chief People Officer at CleanTech Rocks and is a mentor for the CleanTech Quick Start Program, working with students and professionals transitioning into clean tech careers on Long Island. She is also on the Moxxie Emerald Summit Committee, an inaugural event promoting mentoring and leadership at all levels.

She has served as Vice President of the Long Island Chapter of the Alzheimer's Association and President of the Advisory Council for the National Council for the Aging. She served on the Board of the New York Staffing Association and is a past president of the Association of Personnel Consultants, Long Island. In 2008, Gebhardt received The Alternative Board's Most Accomplished Member Award. She is also a recipient of the New York State Jenkins Award for distinguished service to Half Hollow Hills PTA. Gebhardt has been selected twice as one of "Long Island's Most Influential Women" by *Long Island Business News*. In 2009, she was selected as one of *Long Island Business News'* "Inaugural Group of 50 Around 50 or So."

Warning–Disclaimer

While this book strives to provide the reader with practical guidance and to provide general education on the topic at hand, it is not a substitute for adequate legal or other professional advice. The opinions within represent the opinions of the authors and editors only and, therefore, should not be construed as a position on the part of any particular organization or entity.

Further, nothing herein should be construed as the rendering of legal or other professional advice and the reader is advised to consult with appropriate counsel for obtaining any advice. By reading this publication, no attorney client relationship exists between the reader and either the author or publisher.

Introduction

Research has shown that growing industries in science and technology are looking for workers who possess the right skills and that there are approximately twice as many openings as we have workers who can fill those jobs – so, when it comes to your job search your prospects are bright!

We have developed this guide based on our extensive experience in the employment field and to help you through the many aspects of building your career – sharing some of the occupational opportunities and prerequisites to enter those occupations. It will also provide some information about employment trends and wages in the varied careers.

As far as your job search, this guide will address the structure of an effective resume and making the most of the interview process. We have addressed networking and connecting with those in your industry, a practice that, if done well, can be a valuable asset throughout your career. Understanding and participating in social networking is presented in a straight-forward way to allow you to formulate your best strategy for using these tools to your advantage.

Although careers may take very different paths, successful career growth is often predicated on maximizing your exposure to the right opportunities. Although it may only take that one good connection, you can boost the odds of making that connection and creating career opportunities.

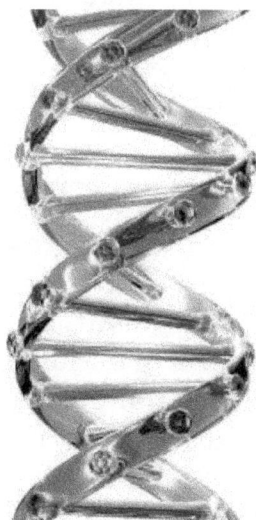

1

Occupational Opportunities in the Scientific Field

T here are many career paths one can take while utilizing their education or experience in the sciences, scientific training or interest in the sciences. The following is a sample of available opportunities in these fields with a brief job description; reported job titles; related job tasks; suggested education, related experience, and job training requirements; related occupations; and national wages and employment trends.

The information that follows was obtained from the Occupational Information Network (O*NET) and O*Net OnLine (www.onetonline.org) and is for informational purposes only. Information and estimates provided are continually updated and are in no way intended to be a guarantee of a job, job offer or salary.

The O*NET program is the nation's primary source of occupational information. Central to the project is the O*NET database, containing information on hundreds of standardized and occupation-specific descriptors. The database, which is available to the public at no cost, is continually updated by surveying a broad range of workers from each occupation. Information from this database forms the heart of O*NET OnLine, an interactive application for exploring and searching occupations

The Occupational Information Network (O*NET) is developed under the sponsorship of the US Department of Labor/Employment and Training Administration (USDOL/ETA) through a grant to the North Carolina Employment Security Commission. The site is maintained by the National Center for O*NET Development, on behalf of the U.S. Department of Labor, Employment and Training Administration (USDOL/ETA).

Please be aware that the accuracy, relevance, timeliness, or completeness of this information is not controlled or guaranteed by O*Net or by the author, Opus Scientific, Opus Staffing, and its affiliates.

☼ Bright Outlook occupations are expected to grow rapidly in the next several years, will have large numbers of job openings, or are new and emerging occupations.

✒ Green occupations will likely change as a result of the green economy. Green economy activities and technologies are increasing the demand for occupations, shaping the work and worker requirements needed for occupational performance, or generating new and emerging occupations.

Agricultural and Food Science Technicians

Work with agricultural and food scientists in food, fiber, and animal research, production, and processing; and assist with animal breeding and nutrition. Conduct tests and experiments to improve yield and quality of crops or to increase the resistance of plants and animals to disease or insects. Includes technicians who assist food scientists or technologists in the research and development of production technology, quality control, packaging, processing, and use of foods.

This title represents a group of more specific occupations. For additional information, please select one of the specific occupations below.

19-4011.01   Agricultural Technicians ✒
19-4011.02   Food Science Technicians

National Wages & Employment Trends:

Median wages (2010)	$15.75 hourly, $32,760 annual
Employment (2008)	22,000 employees

13

Projected growth (2008-2018) Average (7% to 13%)
Projected job openings
(2008-2018) 9,600
Top industries (2008) Educational Services,
 Manufacturing

Agricultural Technicians

Set up or maintain laboratory equipment and collect samples from crops or animals. Prepare specimens or record data to assist scientists in biology or related life science experiments.

Sample of reported job titles: Research Associate, Seed Analyst, Agricultural Research Technician, Laboratory Technician, Research Technician, Research Assistant, Agricultural Research Technologist, County Extension Agent, Technician, Agricultural Laboratory Technician

Tasks

- Receive and prepare laboratory samples for analysis, following proper protocols to ensure that they will be stored, prepared, and disposed of efficiently and effectively.
- Record data pertaining to experimentation, research, or animal care.
- Plant seeds in specified areas, and count the resulting plants to determine the percentage of seeds that germinated.
- Collect samples from crops or animals so testing can be performed.
- Measure or weigh ingredients used in testing or for purposes such as animal feed.

- Prepare data summaries, reports, or analyses that include results, charts, or graphs to document research findings and results.
- Set up laboratory or field equipment, and prepare sites for testing.
- Operate laboratory equipment such as spectrometers, nitrogen determination apparatus, air samplers, centrifuges, and potential hydrogen (pH) meters to perform tests.
- Adjust testing equipment, and prepare culture media, following standard procedures.
- Examine animals and specimens to determine the presence of diseases or other problems.

Education	Most occupations in this zone require training in vocational schools, related on-the-job experience, or an associate's degree.
Related Experience	Previous work-related skill, knowledge, or experience is required for these occupations. For example, an electrician must have completed three or four years of apprenticeship or several years of vocational training, and often must have passed a licensing exam, in order to perform the job.
Job Training	Employees in these occupations usually need one or two years of training involving both on-the-job experience and informal training with experienced workers. A recognized apprenticeship program may be associated with these occupations.

This occupation may require a background in the following science, technology, engineering, and mathematics (STEM) educational disciplines:

Life Sciences — Agricultural Animal Breeding; Agronomy and Crop Science; Animal Sciences; Animal Sciences, General; Dairy Science; Food Science and Technology

Related Occupations:

19-1023.00	Zoologists and Wildlife Biologists
39-2021.00	Nonfarm Animal Caretakers
45-2021.00	Animal Breeders

National Wages & Employment Trends:

Median wages data collected from Agricultural and Food Science Technicians.
Employment data collected from Agricultural and Food Science Technicians.
Industry data collected from Agricultural and Food Science Technicians.

Median wages (2010)	$15.75 hourly, $32,760 annual
Employment (2008)	22,000 employees
Projected growth (2008-2018)	Average (7% to 13%)
Projected job openings (2008-2018)	9,600
Top industries (2008)	Educational Services, Manufacturing

Animal Scientists

Conduct research in the genetics, nutrition, reproduction, growth, and development of domestic farm animals.

Sample of reported job titles: Animal Nutritionist, Animal Scientist, Beef Cattle Specialist, Research and Development Director, Animal Management Systems Specialist, Animal Nutrition Consultant, Animal

Science Section Leader, Beef Cattle Nutritionist, Beef Technical Services Manager, Dairy Consultant

Tasks

- Communicate research findings to the scientific community, producers, and the public.
- Study effects of management practices, processing methods, feed, or environmental conditions on quality and quantity of animal products, such as eggs and milk.
- Conduct research concerning animal nutrition, breeding, or management to improve products or processes.
- Study nutritional requirements of animals and nutritive values of animal feed materials.
- Advise producers about improved products and techniques that could enhance their animal production efforts.
- Research and control animal selection and breeding practices to increase production efficiency and improve animal quality.
- Develop improved practices in feeding, housing, sanitation, or parasite and disease control of animals.
- Crossbreed animals with existing strains or cross strains to obtain new combinations of desirable characteristics.
- Determine genetic composition of animal populations and heritability of traits, utilizing principles of genetics.

Education   Most of these occupations require graduate school. For example, they may require a master's degree, and some require a Ph.D., M.D., or J.D. (law degree).

Related Experience	Extensive skill, knowledge, and experience are needed for these occupations. Many require more than five years of experience. For example, surgeons must complete four years of college and an additional five to seven years of specialized medical training to be able to do their job.
Job Training	Employees may need some on-the-job training, but most of these occupations assume that the person will already have the required skills, knowledge, work-related experience, and/or training.

This occupation may require a background in the following science, technology, engineering, and mathematics (STEM) educational disciplines:

Life Sciences — Agricultural Animal Breeding; Agriculture, General; Animal Sciences; Animal Sciences, General; Dairy Science; Poultry Science

Related Occupations:

19-1013.00	Soil and Plant Scientists
19-1020.01	Biologists
19-4011.01	Agricultural Technicians
29-1031.00	Dietitians and Nutritionists
45-1011.06	First-Line Supervisors of Aquacultural Workers
45-2021.00	Animal Breeders

National Wages & Employment Trends:

Median wages (2010)	$28.00 hourly, $58,250 annual
Employment (2008)	4,000 employees
Projected growth (2008-2018)	Average (7% to 13%)

18

Projected job openings (2008-2018)	1,800
Top industries (2008)	Educational Services, Government

Biochemists and Biophysicists

Study the chemical composition or physical principles of living cells and organisms, their electrical and mechanical energy, and related phenomena. May conduct research to further understanding of the complex chemical combinations and reactions involved in metabolism, reproduction, growth, and heredity. May determine the effects of foods, drugs, serums, hormones, and other substances on tissues and vital processes of living organisms.

Sample of reported job titles: Scientist, Research Scientist, Research Associate, Research Assistant, Analytical Research Chemist, Laboratory Director, Process Engineer, Research Affiliate, Research Chemist

Tasks

- Prepare reports and recommendations based upon research outcomes.
- Develop new methods to study the mechanisms of biological processes.
- Manage laboratory teams, and monitor the quality of a team's work.
- Share research findings by writing scientific articles and by making presentations at scientific conferences.
- Develop and execute tests to detect diseases, genetic disorders, or other abnormalities.

- Develop and test new drugs and medications intended for commercial distribution.
- Study the mutations in organisms that lead to cancer and other diseases.
- Study spatial configurations of submicroscopic molecules such as proteins, using x-rays and electron microscopes.
- Study the chemistry of living processes, such as cell development, breathing and digestion, and living energy changes such as growth, aging, and death.
- Determine the three-dimensional structure of biological macromolecules.

Education	Most of these occupations require graduate school. For example, they may require a master's degree, and some require a Ph.D., M.D., or J.D. (law degree).
Related Experience	Extensive skill, knowledge, and experience are needed for these occupations. Many require more than five years of experience. For example, surgeons must complete four years of college and an additional five to seven years of specialized medical training to be able to do their job.
Job Training	Employees may need some on-the-job training, but most of these occupations assume that the person will already have the required skills, knowledge, work-related experience, and/or training.

This occupation may require a background in the following science, technology, engineering, and mathematics (STEM) educational disciplines:

Chemistry — Soil Chemistry and Physics
Life Sciences — Biochemistry; Biophysics; Cell/Cellular Biology and Anatomical Sciences; Cell/Cellular Biology and Anatomical Sciences, Other; Soil Sciences
Physics/Astronomy — Soil Chemistry and Physics

Related Occupations:

19-1013.00	Soil and Plant Scientists ✦
19-1020.01	Biologists ✦
19-1022.00	Microbiologists
19-1031.01	Soil and Water Conservationists ✦
19-1032.00	Foresters
19-2041.00	Environmental Scientists and Specialists, Including Health ✦ ✦
19-2042.00	Geoscientists, Except Hydrologists and Geographers ✦
19-4011.02	Food Science Technicians
19-4021.00	Biological Technicians

National Wages & Employment Trends:

Median wages (2010)	$38.17 hourly, $79,390 annual
Employment (2008)	23,000 employees
Projected growth (2008-2018)	Much faster than average (20% or higher)
Projected job openings (2008-2018)	16,200
Top industries (2008)	Professional, Scientific, and Technical Services, Manufacturing

Bioinformatics Scientists

Conduct research using bioinformatics theory and methods in areas such as pharmaceuticals, medical technology, biotechnology, computational biology, proteomics, computer information science, biology and medical informatics. May design databases and develop algorithms for processing and analyzing genomic information, or other biological information.

This title represents an occupation for which additional data collection is currently underway.

Tasks

- Analyze large molecular datasets such as raw microarray data, genomic sequence data, and proteomics data for clinical or basic research purposes.
- Consult with researchers to analyze problems, recommend technology-based solutions, or determine computational strategies.
- Manipulate publicly accessible, commercial, or proprietary genomic, proteomic, or post-genomic databases.
- Communicate research results through conference presentations, scientific publications, or project reports.
- Compile data for use in activities such as gene expression profiling, genome annotation, and structural bioinformatics.
- Create novel computational approaches and analytical tools as required by research goals.
- Create or modify web-based bioinformatics tools.
- Design and apply bioinformatics algorithms including unsupervised and supervised machine learning, dynamic programming, or graphic algorithms.
- Develop data models and databases.
- Develop new software applications or customize existing applications to meet specific scientific project needs.

National Wages & Employment Trends:

Median wages data collected from Biological Scientists, All Other. Employment data collected from Biological Scientists, All Other.

Industry data collected from Biological Scientists, All Other.

Median wages (2010)	$32.80 hourly, $68,220 annual
Employment (2008)	32,000 employees
Projected growth (2008-2018)	Faster than average (14% to 19%)
Projected job openings (2008-2018)	16,100
Top industries (2008)	Government, Educational Services

Biological Scientists, All Other

All biological scientists not listed separately.

"All Other" titles represent occupations with a wide range of characteristics which do not fit into one of the detailed O*NET-SOC occupations. O*NET data is not available for this type of title. For more detailed occupations under this title, see below.

19-1029.01   Bioinformatics Scientists ☼
19-1029.02   Molecular and Cellular Biologists ☼
19-1029.03   Geneticists ☼

National Wages & Employment Trends:

Median wages (2010)	$32.80 hourly, $68,220 annual
Employment (2008)	32,000 employees
Projected growth (2008-2018)	Faster than average (14% to 19%)
Projected job openings (2008-2018)	16,100
Top industries (2008)	Government, Educational Services

Biological Technicians

Assist biological and medical scientists in laboratories. Set up, operate, and maintain laboratory instruments and equipment, monitor experiments, make observations, and calculate and record results. May analyze organic substances, such as blood, food, and drugs.

Sample of reported job titles: Biological Technician, Research Associate, Laboratory Technician, Biological Science Laboratory Technician, Research Specialist, Research Assistant, Research Technician, Environmental Technician, Resource Biologist, Wildlife Biology Technician

Tasks

- Conduct research or assist in the conduct of research, including the collection of information and samples, such as blood, water, soil, plants and animals.
- Analyze experimental data and interpret results to write reports and summaries of findings.
- Keep detailed logs of all work-related activities.
- Use computers, computer-interfaced equipment, robotics or high-technology industrial applications to perform work duties.
- Clean, maintain and prepare supplies and work areas.
- Set up, adjust, calibrate, clean, maintain, and troubleshoot laboratory and field equipment.
- Measure or weigh compounds and solutions for use in testing or animal feed.
- Isolate, identify and prepare specimens for examination.

- Conduct standardized biological, microbiological or biochemical tests and laboratory analyses to evaluate the quantity or quality of physical or chemical substances in food or other products.
- Examine animals and specimens to detect the presence of disease or other problems.

Education	Most of these occupations require a four-year bachelor's degree, but some do not.
Related Experience	A considerable amount of work-related skill, knowledge, or experience is needed for these occupations. For example, an accountant must complete four years of college and work for several years in accounting to be considered qualified.
Job Training	Employees in these occupations usually need several years of work-related experience, on-the-job training, and/or vocational training.

There are four recognized apprenticeable specialties associated with this occupation: Dairy Technologist; Bio-Manufacturing Technician (Upstream); Bio-Manufacturing Technician (Downstream); Microbiology Quality Control Technician

To learn about specific apprenticeship opportunities, please consult the U.S. Department of Labor State Apprenticeship Information website (http://www.doleta. gov/oa/sainformation.cfm).

For general information about apprenticeships, training, and partnerships with business, visit the U.S.

Department of Labor Office of Apprenticeship website (http://www.doleta.gov/oa/).

Related Occupations:

19-1031.01	Soil and Water Conservationists *◢*
19-1032.00	Foresters
29-1031.00	Dietitians and Nutritionists
29-1061.00	Anesthesiologists ⚙
29-1081.00	Podiatrists
29-1131.00	Veterinarians ⚙
29-2011.00	Medical and Clinical Laboratory Technologists

National Wages & Employment Trends:

Median wages (2010)	$18.76 hourly, $39,020 annual
Employment (2008)	80,000 employees
Projected growth (2008-2018)	Faster than average (14% to 19%)
Projected job openings (2008-2018)	41,900
Top industries (2008)	Educational Services, Professional, Scientific, and Technical Services

Biologists

Research or study basic principles of plant and animal life, such as origin, relationship, development, anatomy, and functions.

Sample of reported job titles: Scientist, Biologist, Environmental Analyst, Research Scientist, Environmental Specialist, Fisheries Biologist, Research Biologist, Aquatic Scientist, Assistant Scientist, Marine Biologist

Tasks

- Collect and analyze biological data about relationships among and between organisms and their environment.
- Supervise biological technicians and technologists and other scientists.
- Program and use computers to store, process and analyze data.
- Prepare technical and research reports such as environmental impact reports, and communicate the results to individuals in industry, government, or the general public.
- Develop and maintain liaisons and effective working relations with groups and individuals, agencies, and the public to encourage cooperative management strategies or to develop information and interpret findings.
- Prepare requests for proposals or statements of work.
- Represent employer in a technical capacity at conferences.
- Study and manage wild animal populations.
- Study aquatic plants and animals and environmental conditions affecting them such as radioactivity or pollution.
- Study basic principles of plant and animal life such as origin, relationship, development, anatomy, and function.

Education	Most of these occupations require graduate school. For example, they may require a master's degree, and some require a Ph.D., M.D., or J.D. (law degree).
Related Experience	Extensive skill, knowledge, and experience are needed for these occupations. Many require more than five years of experience. For example,

surgeons must complete four years of college and an additional five to seven years of specialized medical training to be able to do their job.

Job Training   Employees may need some on-the-job training, but most of these occupations assume that the person will already have the required skills, knowledge, work-related experience, and/or training.

This occupation may require a background in the following science, technology, engineering, and mathematics (STEM) educational disciplines:

Life Sciences — Anatomy; Animal Genetics; Animal Physiology; Aquatic Biology/Limnology; Biochemistry; Biological and Biomedical Sciences, Other

Related Occupations

19-1013.00	Soil and Plant Scientists
19-1021.00	Biochemists and Biophysicists
19-1022.00	Microbiologists
19-1023.00	Zoologists and Wildlife Biologists
19-2041.00	Environmental Scientists and Specialists, Including Health

National Wages & Employment Trends:

Median wages data collected from Life, Physical, and Social Science Occupations.
Employment data collected from Biological Scientists.
Industry data collected from Biological Scientists.

Median wages (2010)	$28.14 hourly, $58,530 annual
Employment (2008)	91,000 employees
Projected growth (2008-2018)	Much faster than average (20% or higher)

| Projected job openings (2008-2018) | 48,500 |
| Top industries (2008) | Government, Professional, Scientific, and Technical Services |

Chemical Technicians

Conduct chemical and physical laboratory tests to assist scientists in making qualitative and quantitative analyses of solids, liquids, and gaseous materials for research and development of new products or processes, quality control, maintenance of environmental standards, and other work involving experimental, theoretical, or practical application of chemistry and related sciences.

Sample of reported job titles: Laboratory Technician (Lab Tech), Laboratory Analyst (Lab Analyst), Research Technician, Analytical Lab Technician, Laboratory Tester (Lab Tester), Research and Development Technician, Analytical Technician, Chemical Technician, Environmental Lab Technician, Formulation Technician

Tasks

- Monitor product quality to ensure compliance with standards and specifications.
- Compile and interpret results of tests and analyses.
- Set up and conduct chemical experiments, tests, and analyses, using techniques such as chromatography, spectroscopy, physical or chemical separation techniques, or microscopy.

- Conduct chemical or physical laboratory tests to assist scientists in making qualitative or quantitative analyses of solids, liquids, or gaseous materials.
- Provide and maintain a safe work environment by participating in safety programs, committees, or teams and by conducting laboratory or plant safety audits.
- Prepare chemical solutions for products or processes, following standardized formulas, or create experimental formulas.
- Maintain, clean, or sterilize laboratory instruments or equipment.
- Write technical reports or prepare graphs or charts to document experimental results.
- Provide technical support or assistance to chemists or engineers.
- Order and inventory materials to maintain supplies.

Education	Most occupations in this zone require training in vocational schools, related on-the-job experience, or an associate's degree.
Related Experience	Previous work-related skill, knowledge, or experience is required for these occupations. For example, an electrician must have completed three or four years of apprenticeship or several years of vocational training, and often must have passed a licensing exam, in order to perform the job.
Job Training	Employees in these occupations usually need one or two years of training involving both on-the-job experience and informal training with experienced workers. A recognized apprenticeship program may be associated with these occupations.

There are five recognized apprenticeable specialties associated with this occupation: Chemical Laboratory Technician; Laboratory Technician; Laboratory Tester; Chemical-Engineering Technician; Chemistry Quality Control Technician

To learn about specific apprenticeship opportunities, please consult the U.S. Department of Labor State Apprenticeship Information website (http://www.doleta. gov/oa/sainformation.cfm).

For general information about apprenticeships, training, and partnerships with business, visit the U.S. Department of Labor Office of Apprenticeship website (http://www.doleta.gov/oa/).

Related Occupations:

19-1013.00	Soil and Plant Scientists ✐
19-2031.00	Chemists ✐
19-4011.02	Food Science Technicians
19-4091.00	Environmental Science and Protection Technicians, Including Health ✿ ✐
37-2021.00	Pest Control Workers
51-9011.00	Chemical Equipment Operators and Tenders ✐

National Wages & Employment Trends:

Median wages (2010)	$20.21 hourly, $42,040 annual
Employment (2008)	66,000 employees
Projected growth (2008-2018)	Little or no change (-2% to 2%)
Projected job openings (2008-2018)	13,300
Top industries (2008)	Manufacturing Professional, Scientific, and Technical Services

31

Chemists

Conduct qualitative and quantitative chemical analyses or experiments in laboratories for quality or process control or to develop new products or knowledge.

Sample of reported job titles: Chemist, Research Chemist, Air Quality Chemist, Analytical Chemist, Scientist, Sanitary Chemist, Product Development Chemist, Quality Control Chemist, Analytical Specialist, Environmental Chemist

Tasks

- Analyze organic or inorganic compounds to determine chemical or physical properties, composition, structure, relationships, or reactions, using chromatography, spectroscopy, or spectrophotometry techniques.
- Maintain laboratory instruments to ensure proper working order and troubleshoot malfunctions when needed.
- Develop, improve, or customize products, equipment, formulas, processes, or analytical methods.
- Conduct quality control tests.
- Direct, coordinate, or advise personnel in test procedures for analyzing components or physical properties of materials.
- Prepare test solutions, compounds, or reagents for laboratory personnel to conduct tests.
- Compile and analyze test information to determine process or equipment operating efficiency or to diagnose malfunctions.

- Confer with scientists or engineers to conduct analyses of research projects, interpret test results, or develop nonstandard tests.
- Write technical papers or reports or prepare standards and specifications for processes, facilities, products, or tests.
- Induce changes in composition of substances by introducing heat, light, energy, or chemical

Education	Most of these occupations require a four-year bachelor's degree, but some do not.
Related Experience	A considerable amount of work-related skill, knowledge, or experience is needed for these occupations. For example, an accountant must complete four years of college and work for several years in accounting to be considered qualified.
Job Training	Employees in these occupations usually need several years of work-related experience, on-the-job training, and/or vocational training.

This occupation may require a background in the following science, technology, engineering, and mathematics (STEM) educational disciplines:

Chemistry — Analytical Chemistry; Chemical Physics; Chemistry; Inorganic Chemistry; Organic Chemistry; Physical and Theoretical Chemistry
Physics/Astronomy — Chemical Physics

Related Occupations:

19-1013.00	Soil and Plant Scientists ✒
19-2032.00	Materials Scientists ✒
19-4011.02	Food Science Technicians
19-4031.00	Chemical Technicians ✒

19-4091.00   Environmental Science and Protection Technicians, Including Health

51-8091.00   Chemical Plant and System Operators

National Wages & Employment Trends:

Median wages (2010)	$32.85 hourly, $68,320 annual
Employment (2008)	84,000 employees
Projected growth (2008-2018)	Little or no change (-2% to 2%)
Projected job openings (2008-2018)	30,000
Top industries (2008)	Manufacturing
	Professional, Scientific, and Technical Services

Environmental Science and Protection Technicians, Including Health

Perform laboratory and field tests to monitor the environment and investigate sources of pollution, including those that affect health, under the direction of an environmental scientist, engineer, or other specialist. May collect samples of gases, soil, water, and other materials for testing.

Sample of reported job titles: Environmental Technician, Environmental Specialist, Laboratory Specialist, Process Laboratory Specialist, Environmental Health Specialist, Laboratory Technician, Sanitarian, Public Health Sanitarian, Industrial Pretreatment Program Specialist (IPP Specialist), Sanitarian Specialist

Tasks

- Collect samples of gases, soils, water, industrial wastewater, or asbestos products to conduct tests on pollutant levels or identify sources of pollution. ✐
- Record test data and prepare reports, summaries, or charts that interpret test results. ✐
- Develop or implement programs for monitoring of environmental pollution or radiation. ✐
- Discuss test results and analyses with customers. ✐
- Set up equipment or stations to monitor and collect pollutants from sites, such as smoke stacks, manufacturing plants, or mechanical equipment. ✐
- Maintain files, such as hazardous waste databases, chemical usage data, personnel exposure information, or diagrams showing equipment locations. ✐
- Develop testing procedures or direct activities of workers in laboratory. ✐
- Prepare samples or photomicrographs for testing and analysis. ✐
- Calibrate microscopes or test instruments. ✐
- Examine and analyze material for presence and concentration of contaminants, such as asbestos, using variety of microscopes. ✐

Education	Most of these occupations require a four-year bachelor's degree, but some do not.
Related Experience	A considerable amount of work-related skill, knowledge, or experience is needed for these occupations. For example, an accountant must complete four years of college and work for several years in accounting to be considered qualified.

Job Training Employees in these occupations usually need several years of work-related experience, on-the-job training,
and/or vocational training.

There is one recognized apprenticeable specialty associated with this occupation: Laboratory Assistant

To learn about specific apprenticeship opportunities,
please consult the U.S. Department of Labor State Apprenticeship Information website (http://www.doleta.
gov/oa/sainformation.cfm).

For general information about apprenticeships, training, and partnerships with business, visit the U.S. Department of Labor Office of Apprenticeship website
(http://www.doleta.gov/oa/).

This occupation may require a background in the following science, technology, engineering, and mathematics
(STEM) educational disciplines:

Environmental Science — Environmental Science; Environmental Studies; Physical Science Technologies/Techni-
cians, Other

Related Occupations:

13-1041.01	Environmental Compliance Inspectors ☼
19-1013.00	Soil and Plant Scientists 🖊
19-2031.00	Chemists 🖊
19-4011.02	Food Science Technicians
19-4031.00	Chemical Technicians 🖊
19-4092.00	Forensic Science Technicians ☼
29-9011.00	Occupational Health and Safety Specialists 🖊
51-9011.00	Chemical Equipment Operators and Tenders 🖊

National Wages & Employment Trends:

Median wages (2010)	$19.90 hourly, $41,380 annual
Employment (2008)	35,000 employees
Projected growth (2008-2018)	Much faster than average (20% or higher)
Projected job openings (2008-2018)	25,200
Top industries (2008)	Professional, Scientific, and Technical Services, Government

---

Environmental Scientists and Specialists, Including Health

Conduct research or perform investigation for the purpose of identifying, abating, or eliminating sources of pollutants or hazards that affect either the environment or the health of the population. Using knowledge of various scientific disciplines, may collect, synthesize, study, report, and recommend action based on data derived from measurements or observations of air, food, soil, water, and other sources.

Sample of reported job titles: Environmental Scientist, Environmental Specialist, Environmental Analyst, Environmental Protection Specialist, Hazardous Substances Scientist, Environmental Health and Safety Specialist, Environmental Manager, Research Environmental Scientist, Environmental Affairs Specialist, Environmental Health Specialist

Also see: Climate Change Analysts, Environmental Restoration Planners, Industrial Ecologists

Tasks

- Collect, synthesize, analyze, manage, and report environmental data, such as pollution emission measurements, atmospheric monitoring measurements, meteorological or mineralogical information, or soil or water samples.
- Analyze data to determine validity, quality, and scientific significance and to interpret correlations between human activities and environmental effects.
- Communicate scientific or technical information to the public, organizations, or internal audiences through oral briefings, written documents, workshops, conferences, training sessions, or public hearings.
- Provide scientific or technical guidance, support, coordination, or oversight to governmental agencies, environmental programs, industry, or the public.
- Process and review environmental permits, licenses, or related materials.
- Review and implement environmental technical standards, guidelines, policies, and formal regulations that meet all appropriate requirements.
- Prepare charts or graphs from data samples, providing summary information on the environmental relevance of the data.
- Determine data collection methods to be employed in research projects or surveys.
- Investigate and report on accidents affecting the environment.
- Research sources of pollution to determine their effects on the environment and to develop theories or methods of pollution abatement or control.

Education	Most of these occupations require a four-year bachelor's degree, but some do not.
Related Experience	A considerable amount of work-related skill, knowledge, or experience is

	needed for these occupations. For example, an accountant must complete four years of college and work for several years in accounting to be considered qualified.
Job Training	Employees in these occupations usually need several years of work-related experience, on-the-job training, and/or vocational training.

There is one recognized apprenticeable specialty associated with this occupation: Environmental Analyst

To learn about specific apprenticeship opportunities, please consult the U.S. Department of Labor State Apprenticeship Information website (http://www.doleta. gov/oa/sainformation.cfm).

For general information about apprenticeships, training, and partnerships with business, visit the U.S. Department of Labor Office of Apprenticeship website (http://www.doleta.gov/oa/).

This occupation may require a background in the following science, technology, engineering, and mathematics (STEM) educational disciplines:

Environmental Science — Environmental Science; Environmental Studies

Related Occupations:

19-1020.01	Biologists ✿
19-1021.00	Biochemists and Biophysicists ✿
19-1022.00	Microbiologists

19-1032.00   Foresters
19-4011.02   Food Science Technicians

National Wages & Employment Trends:

Median wages (2010)	$29.66 hourly, $61,700 annual
Employment (2008)	86,000 employees
Projected growth (2008-2018)	Much faster than average (20% or higher)
Projected job openings (2008-2018)	48,400
Top industries (2008)	Government Professional, Scientific, and Technical Services

Epidemiologists

Investigate and describe the determinants and distribution of disease, disability, or health outcomes. May develop the means for prevention and control.

Sample of reported job titles: Epidemiologist, Nurse Epidemiologist, Infection Control Practitioner (ICP), Epidemiology Investigator, Research Epidemiologist, Chronic Disease Epidemiologist, Communicable Disease Specialist, Epidemiologist Advanced, State Epidemiologist, Environmental Epidemiologist

Tasks

- Monitor and report incidents of infectious diseases to local and state health agencies.
- Plan and direct studies to investigate human or animal disease, preventive methods, and treatments for disease.

- Communicate research findings on various types of diseases to health practitioners, policy makers, and the public.
- Provide expertise in the design, management and evaluation of study protocols and health status questionnaires, sample selection and analysis.
- Oversee public health programs, including statistical analysis, health care planning, surveillance systems, and public health improvement.
- Investigate diseases or parasites to determine cause and risk factors, progress, life cycle, or mode of transmission.
- Educate healthcare workers, patients, and the public about infectious and communicable diseases, including disease transmission and prevention.
- Conduct research to develop methodologies, instrumentation and procedures for medical application, analyzing data and presenting findings.
- Identify and analyze public health issues related to foodborne parasitic diseases and their impact on public policies or scientific studies or surveys.
- Supervise professional, technical and clerical personnel.

Education	Most of these occupations require graduate school. For example, they may require a master's degree, and some require a Ph.D., M.D., or J.D. (law degree).
Related Experience	Extensive skill, knowledge, and experience are needed for these occupations. Many require more than five years of experience. For example, surgeons must complete four years of college and an additional five to seven years of specialized medical training to be able to do their job.
Job Training	Employees may need some on-the-job training, but most of these

occupations assume that the person will already have the required skills, knowledge, work-related experience, and/or training.

This occupation may require a background in the following science, technology, engineering, and mathematics (STEM) educational disciplines:

Life Sciences — Biophysics; Cell/Cellular Biology and Anatomical Sciences; Cell/Cellular Biology and Histology; Epidemiology

Related Occupations:

19-1031.01	Soil and Water Conservationists
19-1032.00	Foresters
29-1031.00	Dietitians and Nutritionists
29-1061.00	Anesthesiologists
29-1081.00	Podiatrists
29-1131.00	Veterinarians
29-2011.00	Medical and Clinical Laboratory Technologists

National Wages & Employment Trends:

Median wages (2010)	$30.29 hourly, $63,010 annual
Employment (2008)	5,000 employees
Projected growth (2008-2018)	Faster than average (14% to 19%)
Projected job openings (2008-2018)	1,700
Top industries (2008)	Government Health Care and Social Assistance

Food Science Technicians

Perform standardized qualitative and quantitative tests to determine physical or chemical properties of food or beverage products.

Sample of reported job titles: Laboratory Technician (Lab Technician), Quality Assurance Technician (QA Technician), Quality Control Technician (QC Technician), Quality Assurance Analyst (QA Analyst), Quality Assurance Manager (QA Manager), Quality Assurance Inspector (QA Inspector), Quality Assurance Supervisor (QA Supervisor), Quality Assurance Laboratory Technician (QA Laboratory Technician), Operations Technician, Technical Services Analyst

Tasks

- Conduct standardized tests on food, beverages, additives, or preservatives to ensure compliance with standards and regulations regarding factors such as color, texture, or nutrients.
- Provide assistance to food scientists or technologists in research and development, production technology, or quality control.
- Compute moisture or salt content, percentages of ingredients, formulas, or other product factors, using mathematical and chemical procedures.
- Record or compile test results or prepare graphs, charts, or reports.
- Clean and sterilize laboratory equipment.
- Analyze test results to classify products or compare results with standard tables.
- Taste or smell foods or beverages to ensure that

flavors meet specifications or to select samples with specific characteristics.

- Examine chemical or biological samples to identify cell structures or to locate bacteria or extraneous material, using a microscope.
- Mix, blend, or cultivate ingredients to make reagents or to manufacture food or beverage products.
- Measure, test, or weigh bottles, cans, or other containers to ensure that hardness, strength, or dimensions meet specifications.

Education	Similar occupations require training in vocational schools, related on-the-job experience, or an associate's degree.
Related Experience	Previous work-related skill, knowledge, or experience is required for these occupations. For example, an electrician must have completed three or four years of apprenticeship or several years of vocational training, and often must have passed a licensing exam, in order to perform the job.
Job Training	Employees in these occupations usually need one or two years of training involving both on-the-job experience and informal training with experienced workers. A recognized apprenticeship program may be associated with these occupations.

This occupation may require a background in the following science, technology, engineering, and mathematics (STEM) educational disciplines:

Life Sciences — Agricultural Animal Breeding; Animal Sciences; Animal Sciences, General; Dairy Science; Food Science and Technology

Related Occupations:

19-1013.00	Soil and Plant Scientists ✦
19-1021.00	Biochemists and Biophysicists ☼
19-1022.00	Microbiologists
19-2041.00	Environmental Scientists and Specialists, Including Health ☼ ✦
19-4031.00	Chemical Technicians ✦
19-4091.00	Environmental Science and Protection Technicians, Including Health ☼ ✦

National Wages & Employment Trends:

Median wages data collected from Agricultural and Food Science Technicians.
Employment data collected from Agricultural and Food Science Technicians.
Industry data collected from Agricultural and Food Science Technicians.

Median wages (2010)	$15.75 hourly, $32,760 annual
Employment (2008)	22,000 employees
Projected growth (2008-2018)	Average (7% to 13%)
Projected job openings (2008-2018)	9,600
Top industries (2008)	Educational Services, Manufacturing

Food Scientists and Technologists

Use chemistry, microbiology, engineering, and other sciences to study the principles underlying the processing and deterioration of foods; analyze food content to determine levels of vitamins, fat, sugar, and protein; discover new food sources; research ways to make

45

processed foods safe, palatable, and healthful; and apply food science knowledge to determine best ways to process, package, preserve, store, and distribute food.

Sample of reported job titles: Food Technologist, Food Scientist, Quality Assurance Manager (QA Manager), Professor, Product Development Manager, Research and Development Director (R & D Director), Research and Development Manager (R & D Manager), Research Scientist, Food Science Professor, Product Development Scientist

Tasks

- Check raw ingredients for maturity or stability for processing and finished products for safety, quality, and nutritional value.
- Confer with process engineers, plant operators, flavor experts, and packaging and marketing specialists to resolve problems in product development.
- Develop new or improved ways of preserving, processing, packaging, storing, and delivering foods, using knowledge of chemistry, microbiology, and other sciences.
- Develop new food items for production, based on consumer feedback.
- Develop food standards and production specifications, safety and sanitary regulations, and waste management and water supply specifications.
- Inspect food processing areas to ensure compliance with government regulations and standards for sanitation, safety, quality, and waste management standards.
- Search for substitutes for harmful or undesirable additives, such as nitrites.

- Study methods to improve aspects of foods, such as chemical composition, flavor, color, texture, nutritional value, and convenience.
- Demonstrate products to clients.
- Test new products for flavor, texture, color, nutritional content, and adherence to government and industry standards.

Education	Most of these occupations require a four-year bachelor's degree, but some do not.
Related Experience	A considerable amount of work-related skill, knowledge, or experience is needed for these occupations. For example, an accountant must complete four years of college and work for several years in accounting to be considered qualified.
Job Training	Employees in these occupations usually need several years of work-related experience, on-the-job training, and/or vocational training.

This occupation may require a background in the following science, technology, engineering, and mathematics (STEM) educational disciplines:

Life Sciences — Agriculture, General; Food Science and Technology; International Agriculture

Related Occupations:

11-9013.01	Nursery and Greenhouse Managers
11-9013.02	Farm and Ranch Managers ✎
13-1021.00	Buyers and Purchasing Agents, Farm Products ✎
19-4011.02	Food Science Technicians
45-1011.06	First-Line Supervisors of Aquacultural Workers
45-1011.07	First-Line Supervisors of Agricultural Crop and Horticultural Workers ✎

45-1011.08   First-Line Supervisors of Animal Husbandry and
              Animal Care Workers
45-2011.00   Agricultural Inspectors ✒

National Wages & Employment Trends:

Median wages (2010)	$28.93 hourly, $60,180 annual
Employment (2008)	13,000 employees
Projected growth (2008-2018)	Faster than average (14% to 19%)
Projected job openings (2008-2018)	6,900
Top industries (2008)	Manufacturing Professional, Scientific, and Technical Services

---

Geneticists

Research and study the inheritance of traits at the molecular, organism or population level. May evaluate or
treat patients with genetic disorders.

Sample of reported job titles: Professor, Assistant
Professor, Associate Professor, Research Scientist, Associate Professor of Genetics, Clinical Cytogenetics Director, Clinical Molecular Genetics Laboratory Director, Medical Genetics Director

Tasks

- Maintain laboratory notebooks that record research
  methods, procedures, and results.
- Review, approve, or interpret genetic laboratory
  results.
- Plan or conduct basic genomic and biological research
  related to areas such as regulation of gene expression,

protein interactions, metabolic networks, and nucleic acid or protein complexes.

- Search scientific literature to select and modify methods and procedures most appropriate for genetic research goals.
- Write grants and papers or attend fund-raising events to seek research funds.
- Evaluate genetic data by performing appropriate mathematical or statistical calculations and analyses.
- Extract deoxyribonucleic acid (DNA) or perform diagnostic tests involving processes such as gel electrophoresis, Southern blot analysis, and polymerase chain reaction analysis.
- Prepare results of experimental findings for presentation at professional conferences or in scientific journals.
- Attend clinical and research conferences and read scientific literature to keep abreast of technological advances and current genetic research findings.
- Supervise or direct the work of other geneticists, biologists, technicians, or biometricians working on genetics research projects.

Education	Most of these occupations require graduate school. For example, they may require a master's degree, and some require a Ph.D., M.D., or J.D. (law degree).
Related Experience	Extensive skill, knowledge, and experience are needed for these occupations. Many require more than five years of experience. For example, surgeons must complete four years of college and an additional five to seven years of specialized medical training to be able to do their job.
Job Training	Employees may need some on-the-job training, but most of these occupations assume that the person

will already have the required skills, knowledge, work-related experience, and/or training.

This occupation may require a background in the following science, technology, engineering, and mathematics (STEM) educational disciplines:

Life Sciences — Animal Genetics; Human/Medical Genetics; Plant Genetics

National Wages & Employment Trends:

Median wages data collected from Biological Scientists, All Other. Employment data collected from Biological Scientists, All Other. Industry data collected from Biological Scientists, All Other.

Median wages (2010)	$32.80 hourly, $68,220 annual
Employment (2008)	32,000 employees
Projected growth (2008-2018)	Faster than average (14% to 19%)
Projected job openings (2008-2018)	16,100
Top industries (2008)	Government, Educational Services

Hydrologists

Research the distribution, circulation, and physical properties of underground and surface waters; and study the form and intensity of precipitation, its rate of infiltration into the soil, movement through the earth, and its return to the ocean and atmosphere.

Sample of reported job titles: Hydrologist, Hydrogeologist, Professor, Research Hydrologist, Assistant

Groundwater Engineer, Environmental Consultant, Groundwater Consultant, Groundwater Programs Director, Hydraulic Engineer, Hydrologic Engineer

Tasks

- Evaluate data and provide recommendations regarding the feasibility of municipal projects, such as hydroelectric power plants, irrigation systems, flood warning systems, and waste treatment facilities.
- Study and analyze the physical aspects of the earth in terms of the hydrological components, including atmosphere, hydrosphere, and interior structure.
- Administer programs designed to ensure the proper sealing of abandoned wells.
- Install, maintain, and calibrate instruments, such as those that monitor water levels, rainfall, and sediments.
- Answer questions and provide technical assistance and information to contractors or the public regarding issues such as well drilling, code requirements, hydrology, and geology.
- Measure and graph phenomena such as lake levels, stream flows, and changes in water volumes.
- Investigate properties, origins, and activities of glaciers, ice, snow, and permafrost.
- Review applications for site plans and permits and recommend approval, denial, modification, or further investigative action.
- Apply research findings to help minimize the environmental impacts of pollution, waterborne diseases, erosion, and sedimentation.
- Develop or modify methods of conducting hydrologic studies.

Education   Most of these occupations require a four-year bachelor's degree, but some do not.

Related Experience   A considerable amount of work-related skill, knowledge, or experience is needed for these occupations. For example, an accountant must complete four years of college and work for several years in accounting to be considered qualified.

Job Training   Employees in these occupations usually need several years of work-related experience, on-the-job training, and/or vocational training.

This occupation may require a background in the following science, technology, engineering, and mathematics (STEM) educational disciplines:

Geosciences — Geological and Earth Sciences/Geosciences; Geology/Earth Science, General

Related Occupations:

19-2011.00	Astronomers
19-2012.00	Physicists
19-2021.00	Atmospheric and Space Scientists ✍
19-2042.00	Geoscientists, Except Hydrologists and Geographers ✍
19-4041.01	Geophysical Data Technicians ✍
19-4041.02	Geological Sample Test Technicians ✍
51-9083.00	Ophthalmic Laboratory Technicians

National Wages & Employment Trends:

Median wages (2010)	$36.39 hourly, $75,690 annual
Employment (2008)	8,000 employees
Projected growth (2008-2018)	Faster than average (14% to 19%)
Projected job openings (2008-2018)	3,800
Top industries (2008)	Government, Professional, Scientific, and Technical Services

Medical Scientists, Except Epidemiologists

Conduct research dealing with the understanding of human diseases and the improvement of human health. Engage in clinical investigation, research and development, or other related activities. Includes physicians, dentists, public health specialists, pharmacologists, and medical pathologists who primarily conduct research.

Sample of reported job titles: Scientist, Investigator, Laboratory Director, Post-Doctoral Fellow, Research Associate, Clinical Laboratory Scientist, Clinical Pharmacologist, Clinical Research Director, Clinical Research Scientist, Medical Affairs Director

Tasks

- Conduct research to develop methodologies, instrumentation and procedures for medical application, analyzing data and presenting findings.
- Plan and direct studies to investigate human or animal disease, preventive methods, and treatments for disease.
- Follow strict safety procedures when handling toxic materials to avoid contamination.
- Evaluate effects of drugs, gases, pesticides, parasites, and microorganisms at various levels.
- Teach principles of medicine and medical and laboratory procedures to physicians, residents, students, and technicians.
- Prepare and analyze organ, tissue, and cell samples to identify toxicity, bacteria, or microorganisms or to study cell structure.
- Standardize drug dosages, methods of immunization,

and procedures for manufacture of drugs and medicinal compounds.

- Investigate cause, progress, life cycle, or mode of transmission of diseases or parasites.
- Confer with health departments, industry personnel, physicians, and others to develop health safety standards and public health improvement programs.
- Study animal and human health and physiological processes.

Education	Most of these occupations require graduate school. For example, they may require a master's degree, and some require a Ph.D., M.D., or J.D. (law degree).
Related Experience	Extensive skill, knowledge, and experience are needed for these occupations. Many require more than five years of experience. For example, surgeons must complete four years of college and an additional five to seven years of specialized medical training to be able to do their job.
Job Training	Employees may need some on-the-job training, but most of these occupations assume that the person will already have the required skills, knowledge, work-related experience, and/or training.

This occupation may require a background in the following science, technology, engineering, and mathematics (STEM) educational disciplines:

Life Sciences — Anatomy; Biochemistry; Biology, General; Biophysics; Biostatistics; Cell/Cellular Biology and Anatomical Sciences

Related Occupations:

19-1031.01	Soil and Water Conservationists
19-1032.00	Foresters
29-1031.00	Dietitians and Nutritionists
29-1061.00	Anesthesiologists
29-1081.00	Podiatrists
29-1131.00	Veterinarians
29-2011.00	Medical and Clinical Laboratory Technologists

National Wages & Employment Trends:

Median wages (2010)	$36.87 hourly, $76,700 annual
Employment (2008)	109,000 employees
Projected growth (2008-2018)	Much faster than average (20% or higher)
Projected job openings (2008-2018)	66,200
Top industries (2008)	Professional, Scientific, and Technical Services, Educational Services

Microbiologists

Investigate the growth, structure, development, and other characteristics of microscopic organisms, such as bacteria, algae, or fungi. Includes medical microbiologists who study the relationship between organisms and disease or the effects of antibiotics on microorganisms.

Sample of reported job titles: Microbiologist, Microbiological Analyst, Clinical Laboratory Scientist, Bacteriologist, Study Director, Microbiological Laboratory Technician, Microbiology Laboratory Manager, Professor of Microbiology, Quality Control Microbiologist (QC Microbiologist), Clinical Microbiologist

Tasks

- Investigate the relationship between organisms and disease including the control of epidemics and the effects of antibiotics on microorganisms.
- Prepare technical reports and recommendations based upon research outcomes.
- Supervise biological technologists and technicians and other scientists.
- Provide laboratory services for health departments, for community environmental health programs and for physicians needing information for diagnosis and treatment.
- Use a variety of specialized equipment such as electron microscopes, gas chromatographs and high pressure liquid chromatographs, electrophoresis units, thermocyclers, fluorescence activated cell sorters and phosphoimagers.
- Examine physiological, morphological, and cultural characteristics, using microscopes, to identify and classify microorganisms in human, water, and food specimens.
- Study growth, structure, development, and general characteristics of bacteria and other microorganisms to understand their relationship to human, plant, and animal health.
- Isolate and maintain cultures of bacteria or other microorganisms in prescribed or developed media, controlling moisture, aeration, temperature, and nutrition.
- Observe action of microorganisms upon living tissues of plants, higher animals, and other microorganisms, and on dead organic matter.
- Study the structure and function of human, animal and plant tissues, cells, pathogens and toxins.

Education   Most of these occupations require graduate school. For example, they may require a master's degree, and

	some require a Ph.D., M.D., or J.D. (law degree).
Related Experience	Extensive skill, knowledge, and experience are needed for these occupations. Many require more than five years of experience. For example, surgeons must complete four years of college and an additional five to seven years of specialized medical training to be able to do their job.
Job Training	Employees may need some on-the-job training, but most of these occupations assume that the person will already have the required skills, knowledge, work-related experience, and/or training.

This occupation may require a background in the following science, technology, engineering, and mathematics (STEM) educational disciplines:

Life Sciences — Cell/Cellular Biology and Anatomical Sciences; Cell/Cellular Biology and Anatomical Sciences, Other; Microbiological Sciences and Immunology; Soil Sciences

Related Occupations:

19-1020.01	Biologists
19-1021.00	Biochemists and Biophysicists
19-1023.00	Zoologists and Wildlife Biologists
19-2041.00	Environmental Scientists and Specialists, Including Health
19-4011.02	Food Science Technicians
29-2011.00	Medical and Clinical Laboratory Technologists

National Wages & Employment Trends:

Median wages (2010)	$31.69 hourly, $65,920 annual
Employment (2008)	17,000 employees
Projected growth (2008-2018)	Average (7% to 13%)

Projected job openings (2008-2018)	7,500
Top industries (2008)	Government
	Professional, Scientific, and Technical Services

Molecular and Cellular Biologists

Research and study cellular molecules and organelles to understand cell function and organization.

Sample of reported job titles: Professor, Assistant Professor, Associate Professor, Biology Professor, Molecular Biology Professor

Tasks

- Maintain accurate laboratory records and data.
- Design molecular or cellular laboratory experiments, oversee their execution, and interpret results.
- Conduct research on cell organization and function including mechanisms of gene expression, cellular bioinformatics, cell signaling, or cell differentiation.
- Instruct undergraduate and graduate students within the areas of cellular or molecular biology.
- Compile and analyze molecular or cellular experimental data and adjust experimental designs as necessary.
- Prepare reports, manuscripts, and meeting presentations.
- Supervise technical personnel and postdoctoral research fellows.
- Direct, coordinate, organize, or prioritize biological laboratory activities.
- Perform laboratory procedures following protocols including deoxyribonucleic acid (DNA) sequencing,

cloning and extraction, ribonucleic acid (RNA) purification, or gel electrophoresis.
- Develop assays that monitor cell characteristics.

Education	Most of these occupations require graduate school. For example, they may require a master's degree, and some require a Ph.D., M.D., or J.D. (law degree).
Related Experience	Extensive skill, knowledge, and experience are needed for these occupations. Many require more than five years of experience. For example, surgeons must complete four years of college and an additional five to seven years of specialized medical training to be able to do their job.
Job Training	Employees may need some on-the-job training, but most of these occupations assume that the person will already have the required skills, knowledge, work-related experience, and/or training.

This occupation may require a background in the following science, technology, engineering, and mathematics (STEM) educational disciplines:

Life Sciences — Cell/Cellular Biology and Histology; Molecular Biology

National Wages & Employment Trends:

Median wages data collected from Biological Scientists, All Other. Employment data collected from Biological Scientists, All Other. Industry data collected from Biological Scientists, All Other.

Median wages (2010)	$32.80 hourly, $68,220 annual
Employment (2008)	32,000 employees

59

Projected growth (2008-2018)	Faster than average (14% to 19%)
Projected job openings (2008-2018)	16,100
Top industries (2008)	Government, Educational Services

Physical Scientists, All Other

All physical scientists not listed separately.

"All Other" titles represent occupations with a wide range of characteristics which do not fit into one of the detailed O*NET-SOC occupations. O*NET data is not available for this type of title. For more detailed occupations under this title, see below.

19-2099.01   Remote Sensing Scientists and Technologists

National Wages & Employment Trends:

Median wages (2010)	$45.57 hourly, $94,780 annual
Employment (2008)	27,000 employees
Projected growth (2008-2018)	Average (7% to 13%)
Projected job openings (2008-2018)	10,100
Top industries (2008)	Government, Professional, Scientific, and Technical Services

Physicists

Conduct research into physical phenomena, develop theories on the basis of observation and experiments, and devise methods to apply physical laws and theories.

Sample of reported job titles: Health Physicist, Scientist, Research Scientist, Physicist, Research Consultant, Research Physicist, Biophysics Scientist

Tasks

- Perform complex calculations as part of the analysis and evaluation of data, using computers.
- Describe and express observations and conclusions in mathematical terms.
- Analyze data from research conducted to detect and measure physical phenomena.
- Report experimental results by writing papers for scientific journals or by presenting information at scientific conferences.
- Design computer simulations to model physical data so that it can be better understood.
- Collaborate with other scientists in the design, development, and testing of experimental, industrial, or medical equipment, instrumentation, and procedures.
- Direct testing and monitoring of contamination of radioactive equipment, and recording of personnel and plant area radiation exposure data.
- Observe the structure and properties of matter, and the transformation and propagation of energy, using equipment such as masers, lasers, and telescopes, in order to explore and identify the basic principles governing these phenomena.

- Develop theories and laws on the basis of observation and experiments, and apply these theories and laws to problems in areas such as nuclear energy, optics, and aerospace technology.
- Teach physics to students.

Education	Most of these occupations require graduate school. For example, they

	may require a master's degree, and some require a Ph.D., M.D., or J.D. (law degree).
Related Experience	Extensive skill, knowledge, and experience are needed for these occupations. Many require more than five years of experience. For example, surgeons must complete four years of college and an additional five to seven years of specialized medical training to be able to do their job.
Job Training	Employees may need some on-the-job training, but most of these occupations assume that the person will already have the required skills, knowledge, work-related experience, and/or training.

This occupation may require a background in the following science, technology, engineering, and mathematics (STEM) educational disciplines:

Mathematics — Theoretical and Mathematical Physics
Physics/Astronomy — Acoustics; Astronomy and Astrophysics; Astrophysics; Atomic/Molecular Physics; Elementary Particle Physics; Health/Medical Physics

Related Occupations:

17-2151.00	Mining and Geological Engineers, Including Mining Safety Engineers
17-2171.00	Petroleum Engineers
19-2011.00	Astronomers
19-2021.00	Atmospheric and Space Scientists ✒
19-2042.00	Geoscientists, Except Hydrologists and Geographers ✒
19-2043.00	Hydrologists ✒
19-4041.01	Geophysical Data Technicians ✒
25-1054.00	Physics Teachers, Postsecondary

National Wages & Employment Trends:

Median wages (2010)	$51.14 hourly, $106,370 annual
Employment (2008)	16,000 employees
Projected growth (2008-2018)	Faster than average (14% to 19%)
Projected job openings (2008-2018)	6,900
Top industries (2008)	Professional, Scientific, and Technical Services, Government

Quality Control Analysts

Conduct tests to determine quality of raw materials, bulk intermediate and finished products. May conduct stability sample tests.

This title represents an occupation for which data collection is currently underway.

Tasks

- Conduct routine and non-routine analyses of in-process materials, raw materials, environmental samples, finished goods, or stability samples.
- Calibrate, validate, or maintain laboratory equipment.
- Compile laboratory test data and perform appropriate analyses.
- Complete documentation needed to support testing procedures including data capture forms, equipment logbooks, or inventory forms.
- Evaluate analytical methods and procedures to determine how they might be improved.
- Identify quality problems and recommend solutions.
- Interpret test results, compare them to established

63

specifications and control limits, and make recommendations on appropriateness of data for release.
- Investigate or report questionable test results.
- Monitor testing procedures to ensure that all tests are performed according to established item specifications, standard test methods, or protocols.
- Participate in out-of-specification and failure investigations and recommend corrective actions.

National Wages & Employment Trends:

Median wages data collected from Life, Physical, and Social Science Technicians, All Other.
Employment data collected from Life, Physical, and Social Science Technicians, All Other.
Industry data collected from Life, Physical, and Social Science Technicians, All Other.

Median wages (2010)	$20.84 hourly, $43,350 annual
Employment (2008)	65,000 employees
Projected growth (2008-2018)	Average (7% to 13%)
Projected job openings (2008-2018)	36,400
Top industries (2008)	Educational Services, Professional, Scientific, and Technical Services

Soil and Plant Scientists

Conduct research in breeding, physiology, production, yield, and management of crops and agricultural plants or trees, shrubs, and nursery stock, their growth in soils, and control of pests; or study the chemical, physical, biological, and mineralogical composition of soils as they relate to plant or crop growth. May classify and map soils and investigate effects of alternative practices on soil and crop productivity.

Sample of reported job titles: Soil Scientist, Agronomy Research Manager, Crop Nutrition Scientist, Microbiology Soil Scientist, Physical Hydrologist, Research Soil Scientist, Soil Fertility Extension Specialist

Tasks

- Communicate research or project results to other professionals or the public or teach related courses, seminars, or workshops.
- Provide information or recommendations to farmers or other landowners regarding ways in which they can best use land, promote plant growth, or avoid or correct problems such as erosion. ✍
- Investigate responses of soils to specific management practices to determine the use capabilities of soils and the effects of alternative practices on soil productivity.
- Develop methods of conserving or managing soil that can be applied by farmers or forestry companies. ✍
- Conduct experiments to develop new or improved varieties of field crops, focusing on characteristics such as yield, quality, disease resistance, nutritional value, or adaptation to specific soils or climates. ✍
- Investigate soil problems and poor water quality to determine sources and effects. ✍
- Study soil characteristics to classify soils on the basis of factors such as geographic location, landscape position, or soil properties.
- Develop improved measurement techniques, soil conservation methods, soil sampling devices, or related technology. ✍
- Conduct experiments investigating how soil forms, changes, or interacts with land-based ecosystems or living organisms. ✍
- Identify degraded or contaminated soils and develop plans to improve their chemical, biological, or physical characteristics. ✍

Education	Most of these occupations require graduate school. For example, they may require a master's degree, and some require a Ph.D., M.D., or J.D. (law degree).
Related Experience	Extensive skill, knowledge, and experience are needed for these occupations. Many require more than five years of experience. For example, surgeons must complete four years of college and an additional five to seven years of specialized medical training to be able to do their job.
Job Training	Employees may need some on-the-job training, but most of these occupations assume that the person will already have the required skills, knowledge, work-related experience, and/or training.

There is one recognized apprenticeable specialty associated with this occupation: Horticulturist

To learn about specific apprenticeship opportunities, please consult the U.S. Department of Labor State Apprenticeship Information website (http://www.doleta.gov/oa/sainformation.cfm).

For general information about apprenticeships, training, and partnerships with business, visit the U.S. Department of Labor Office of Apprenticeship website (http://www.doleta.gov/oa/).

This occupation may require a background in the following science, technology, engineering, and mathematics (STEM) educational disciplines:

Chemistry — Soil Chemistry and Physics
Life Sciences — Agricultural and Horticultural Plant Breeding; Agriculture, General; Agronomy and Crop Science; Horticultural Science; Plant Sciences, General; Range Science and Management
Physics/Astronomy — Soil Chemistry and Physics

Related Occupations:

19-1011.00	Animal Scientists
19-1020.01	Biologists ☼
19-1021.00	Biochemists and Biophysicists ☼
19-1023.00	Zoologists and Wildlife Biologists ✦
19-1031.01	Soil and Water Conservationists ✦
19-4011.02	Food Science Technicians
45-2011.00	Agricultural Inspectors ✦

National Wages & Employment Trends:

Median wages (2010)	$27.57 hourly, $57,340 annual
Employment (2008)	14,000 employees
Projected growth (2008-2018)	Faster than average (14% to 19%)
Projected job openings (2008-2018)	7,000
Top industries (2008)	Professional, Scientific, and Technical Services, Government

Soil and Water Conservationists

Plan or develop coordinated practices for soil erosion control, soil or water conservation, or sound land use.

Sample of reported job titles: Soil Conservationist, Conservationist, Land Reclamation Specialist, Land Resource Specialist, Environmental Analyst, Resource Conservation Specialist, Resource Conservationist, Erosion Control Specialist, Land Manager, Watershed Program Manager

Tasks

- Calculate or compare efficiencies associated with changing from low-precision irrigation technologies, such as furrow irrigation, to high-precision technologies, such as computer-controlled systems. ✒
- Implement soil or water management techniques, such as nutrient management, erosion control, buffers, or filter strips, in accordance with conservation plans. ✒
- Initiate, schedule, or conduct annual audits or compliance checks of program implementation by local government. ✒
- Enter local soil, water, or other environmental data into adaptive or web-based decision tools to identify appropriate analyses or techniques. ✒

- Evaluate or recommend geographic information systems (GIS) applications to address issues such as surface water quality, groundwater quality, ecological risk assessments, air quality, or environmental contamination. ✒
- Compute design specifications for implementation of conservation practices, using survey or field information technical guides or engineering manuals. ✒
- Compile or interpret biodata to determine extent or type of wetlands or to aid in program formulation. ✒
- Respond to complaints or questions on wetland jurisdiction, providing information or clarification. ✒
- Advise land users, such as farmers or ranchers,

on plans, problems, or alternative conservation
solutions. ✒

• Conduct fact-finding or mediation sessions among
government units, landowners, or other agencies to
resolve disputes. ✒

Education	Most of these occupations require a four-year bachelor's degree, but some do not.
Related Experience	A considerable amount of work-related skill, knowledge, or experience is needed for these occupations. For example, an accountant must complete four years of college and work for several years in accounting to be considered qualified.
Job Training	Employees in these occupations usually need several years of work-related experience, on-the-job training, and/or vocational training.

There is one recognized apprenticeable specialty associated with this occupation: Soil-Conservation Technician

To learn about specific apprenticeship opportunities,
please consult the U.S. Department of Labor State Apprenticeship Information website (http://www.doleta.
gov/oa/sainformation.cfm).

For general information about apprenticeships, training, and partnerships with business, visit the U.S. Department of Labor Office of Apprenticeship website
(http://www.doleta.gov/oa/).

This occupation may require a background in the following science, technology, engineering, and mathematics (STEM) educational disciplines:

Life Sciences — Forest Sciences and Biology; Forestry; Natural Resources and Conservation, Other; Natural Resources Management and Policy; Natural Resources/Conservation, General; Wildlife and Wildlands Science and Management

Related Occupations:

17-1012.00	Landscape Architects ✺
19-1013.00	Soil and Plant Scientists ✐
19-1020.01	Biologists ✺
19-1031.02	Range Managers
19-1032.00	Foresters
19-2041.00	Environmental Scientists and Specialists, Including Health ✺ ✐
33-3031.00	Fish and Game Wardens ✐

National Wages & Employment Trends:

Median wages data collected from Conservation Scientists. Employment data collected from Conservation Scientists. Industry data collected from Conservation Scientists.

Median wages (2010)	$28.51 hourly, $59,310 annual
Employment (2008)	18,000 employees
Projected growth (2008-2018)	Average (7% to 13%)
Projected job openings (2008-2018)	4,100
Top industries (2008)	Government

Zoologists and Wildlife Biologists

Study the origins, behavior, diseases, genetics, and life processes of animals and wildlife. May specialize in wildlife research and management. May collect and analyze biological data to determine the environmental effects of present and potential use of land and water habitats.

Sample of reported job titles: Wildlife Biologist, Zoologist, Fish and Wildlife Biologist, Fisheries Biologist, Fishery Biologist, Wildlife Manager, Aquatic Biologist,

Assistant Research Scientist, Conservation Resources Management Biologist, Environmental Specialist

Tasks

- Study animals in their natural habitats, assessing effects of environment and industry on animals, interpreting findings and recommending alternative operating conditions for industry.
- Inventory or estimate plant and wildlife populations.
- Organize and conduct experimental studies with live animals in controlled or natural surroundings.
- Make recommendations on management systems and planning for wildlife populations and habitat, consulting with stakeholders and the public at large to explore options.
- Disseminate information by writing reports and scientific papers or journal articles, and by making presentations and giving talks for schools, clubs, interest groups and park interpretive programs.
- Study characteristics of animals such as origin, interrelationships, classification, life histories and diseases, development, genetics, and distribution.
- Inform and respond to public regarding wildlife and conservation issues, such as plant identification, hunting ordinances, and nuisance wildlife.
- Coordinate preventive programs to control the outbreak of wildlife diseases.

- Analyze characteristics of animals to identify and classify them.
- Prepare collections of preserved specimens or microscopic slides for species identification and study of development or disease.

Education	Most of these occupations require graduate school. For example, they may require a master's degree, and some require a Ph.D., M.D., or J.D. (law degree).
Related Experience	Extensive skill, knowledge, and experience are needed for these occupations. Many require more than five years of experience. For example, surgeons must complete four years of college and an additional five to seven years of specialized medical training to be able to do their job.
Job Training	Employees may need some on-the-job training, but most of these occupations assume that the person will already have the required skills, knowledge, work-related experience, and/or training.

This occupation may require a background in the following science, technology, engineering, and mathematics (STEM) educational disciplines:

Life Sciences — Animal Physiology; Cell/Cellular Biology and Anatomical Sciences; Cell/Cellular Biology and Anatomical Sciences, Other; Ecology; Entomology; Wildlife and Wildlands Science and Management

Related Occupations:

19-1020.01   Biologists ✿
19-1022.00   Microbiologists

19-4011.01   Agricultural Technicians ✒
31-9096.00   Veterinary Assistants and Laboratory Animal
              Caretakers ✿
45-2021.00   Animal Breeders

National Wages & Employment Trends:

Median wages (2010) $27.61 hourly, $57,430 annual
Employment (2008)   20,000 employees
Projected growth (2008-2018)   Average (7% to 13%)
Projected job openings
(2008-2018)   8,800
Top industries (2008)   Government
                                 Professional, Scientific,
                                 and Technical Services

2

Transitioning from Academia to Industry

T here are many available careers and likelihoods for advancement in both academia and industry that can be very rewarding, each offering unique opportunities and challenges. There are, however, some key differences in academia and the bioscience industry that should be considered when deciding to make a transition.

From a student's viewpoint, the transition from academia to industry may seem difficult. Despite the increasing number of job opportunities in the bioscience industry, it can be difficult for undergraduate or graduate students to obtain even entry-level jobs. There are several steps that you can take to prepare for the transition. You can:

- Take advantage of available resources for training in technical writing and public speaking; take advantage of available resources that can help you in preparing a resume and learning how to interview.
- Work with a skilled and well-connected professional recruiter.
- Research available job opportunities by attending university-sponsored job fairs, attending guest lectures, and researching and visiting local companies.
- Research colleges and companies that can offer specialized training.
- Obtain [additional] experience and training which might include internships or volunteer opportunities.

For those in academia who are interested in transitioning to industry, like any other career decision, you will need to assess your strengths and weaknesses and decide the best fit. Ask yourself these questions:

- What type of environment do you find enjoyable and where do you feel you would thrive?
  - Do you like to work independently or as part of a team?
  - Do you want to run your own lab and be the decision maker? Would you prefer to have a boss who leads the research?
- Do you want to work on a particular project? If you could no longer work on that project, would you still be happy?
- Do you want to write grants?

- Do you want to get published?
- Do you enjoy teaching and working with students?

Some differences between Industry and Academia that you may want to consider include:

Industry:

- Suitable for a goal-oriented personality.
- Tendency toward a team environment and approach – interacting with others at all levels of education and sharing credit and appreciation for the contribution.
- Opportunity for greater income.
- Opportunity for career advancement or development – management, product development or regulatory affairs, for example.
- Research may have a more rapid pace and more direct, immediate and tangible impact.
- Corporate mandates affect both what and how research is done and is typically directed toward a market/product end. Research philosophy centers on company success, financial benefit for the company, employees and shareholders.
- Goals include papers, patents and products.
- Since research can be product driven there may be limited research freedom.
- Research projects may be evaluated against objectives, targeted costs and a timeline. Management may have a tendency to have more control and responsibility.
- Suitable for risk takers, those with the skills for recognizing practical applications of concepts, theories and research, and for those looking for a fit between your existing skills, your general and

specific knowledge, and the job at hand.
- Political struggles.

Academia:

- Suitable for individuals looking for status, prestige, competition, and autonomy.
- Success measured on an individual basis – published papers, fellowships, awards and grants are needed to obtain support for your research.
- Opportunities for research independence, supervisory and influential roles (training students), travel and public contact (speaking at conferences, teaching undergraduates, consulting), and publishing.
- Managerial opportunities for academic researchers as department heads, deans, and provosts appointed by the faculty; focus being on running a department, college or university.
- Requires time devoted to obtaining funding for your work and for the resources needed.
- Research may have a more long-term, indirect impact.
- Suitable for an individual looking for job security – the opportunity to spend a lot of time working on a project; opportunity to create an ambitious, long-term agenda.
- Research is typically self-initiated and self-directed; offers freedom and flexibility to do what you want and set your own agenda.
- Suitable for those with the appropriate people skills and interest in teaching and working in a learning environment.
- Goals include obtaining money, publishing papers, and teaching students.

- Projects can be limited in scale with limited resources.
- Incremental, needs-based approach to acquiring skills; will only need to show that you have the potential to master new research skills as proof of success.

When considering a transition from academia to industry, approach the decision with the analytical skills you've learned. Gather data from all available sources, network with your colleagues, obtain industry newsletters and blogs and organize it systematically. Make a list of pros and cons for each. Assess what you value in your work and what you want out of your career; take a look at your qualifications and consider where you would be best suited and positioned for success.

Keep in mind that as you work through the decision-making process, your priorities may change over time so don't think only about what you might want right now but what you may want or like in the future. Be honest with yourself, and keep some perspective – your choice is important but not necessarily permanent.

3

Resumes

When writing a resume, always keep in mind "you never get a second chance to make a good first impression." Your resume plays an important role in the job search process – the purpose being to attract the attention of the hiring manager and secure an interview. It may be your first contact with a potential employer. It often reaches the hiring authority before you do!

Types of Resumes

A resume tells the prospective employer what you have accomplished in the past and what you can do for their company now. There are several basic types of resume formats that one can use depending on your personal circumstances. The resume styles most widely used are the reverse chronological or the functional. Others (the combination or targeted, for example) are variations or combinations of these. Choose a style that emphasizes your strengths and de-emphasizes your weaknesses. Include examples of results that you produced that benefited your previous employers. Employers want to see measurable achievements.

The Reverse Chronological

One of the more preferred styles, a reverse chronological resume [sometimes] contains an objective or summary statement and then presents your work history in reverse chronological order beginning with your current or most recent job at the top of the list. Your education, skills and other information are presented after your experience. This type of resume works well if your recent job experience is related to the job you are applying for and you are staying on a similar career path.

The reverse chronological resume may not work well if you are just entering the workforce as this may highlight your lack of experience. In addition, if you have held recent jobs that have no relevance to the position you are applying for, if you are re-entering the workforce after a substantial absence, or if you job history shows many briefly held jobs, the reverse chronological resume would not be the appropriate format. With these situations you may want to present your work history in a functional resume style.

To summarize:

Use this style if:

- You have progressed through a clearly defined career path and are looking for continued advancement.
- You have recent experience in the field you are seeking.
- You have a continuous work history in your field.

Do not use this style if:

- You have had many different types of jobs.
- You have changed jobs frequently.
- You are considering switching fields.
- You are just starting out.

The Functional

A functional resume emphasizes your overall skills and experience and highlights your abilities. This style is, again, used most often by individuals who are re-entering the workforce, transitioning into new careers, have frequently changed jobs, or who have had gaps in their recent employment history. Employment history is summarized and skills and relevant experience are presented at the beginning of the resume. Your skills and experience are organized in a way in which the employer can see how they relate to the position you are applying for. This style of resume also works well in situations where one has acquired skills or experiences which may be transferable. These experiences may include volunteer work or internships and might include hiring, managing or coaching skills.

To summarize:

Use this style if:

- You have worked for only one employer, but have performed a wide variety of jobs.
- You are applying for a job that is different from your present or most recent job(s).
- You have little or no job experience or are just starting out. Emphasize activities that demonstrate qualities such as leadership abilities or organization skills.
- You have gaps in your work history.
- You are reentering the job market.

Do not use this style if:

- Your work history is stable and continuous.

Writing Tips

When preparing your resume, keep the following in mind:

- Your resume should be concise, succinct and to the point. Check your resume for proper grammar, spelling, and punctuation which can be evidence of good communication skills and attention to detail.
- Make your words count – your use of language is important – sell yourself quickly and efficiently, addressing needs with a clearly written, compelling resume. A successful resume not only depends on what you say but also how you say it.

- Avoid using long paragraphs and provide small, digestible pieces of information. Also, use strong, action verbs to emphasize accomplishments, such as "developed," "managed," and "designed." Avoid declarative sentences ("I developed ...") and passive constructions ("was responsible for ...").
- Make the most of your experiences and accomplishments – provide details on what you have accomplished without being vague. Describe things that can be measured objectively.
- Be factually accurate, including dates of employment, education completed, jobs title and location, and skills possessed. A falsified resume can often be spotted by an employer, if not immediately then during the interview process.
- Your resume should be visually appealing. Make sure it is neat, organized, and consistent. Again, your resume the first impression you'll make to a potential employer.
- Your resume should also be easy on the eyes and professional looking – Use normal margins and avoid unusual or exotic font styles – use simple, 10 to 12 point fonts with an easy-to-read, professional look.
- Emphasize what you can do for an employer. Be specific and customize accordingly. Your resume and the way it is organized should be relevant to the position you are applying for.
- Eliminate superfluous details – unnecessary details can take up a lot of valuable space on your resume. Don't mention personal characteristics which employers may not legally solicit from you.

Components of a Resume

When preparing your resume, consider the following items:

Contact Information

- Include details of your home address; do not list your work address
- Include a personal email address
- Include home and/or cellular phone number

Summary or Career Objective

- The "Summary" or "Objective" may be an optional component to your resume. It provides direction and focus and should allow an employer to immediately identify the targeted job or field of employment. You may wish to omit an objective if you aren't sure of your career direction at this time.
- In a Summary, clearly communicate the type of job you want and what you can offer the employer. You may want to keep your Summary limited to two or three sentences.
- You can prepare an Objective that is broad enough to include related jobs, but not too broad that you appear unfocused or willing to take any job. Keep your Objective limited to one or two sentences.
- Try not to be too vague or restrictive.
- Be concise but try not to over generalize.
- Avoid phrases such as "challenging, rewarding career."

Education

- List degree(s), college(s) attended, location(s), and date(s) of completion.
- Include major(s), minor(s), and areas of concentration.
- Include certifications, honors, special awards, skill-based training, etc.
- If applicable, include experience studying abroad.
- It may not be necessary to include high school information, depending on your level of education and/or extent of work experience.

Related Work Experience

- Provide details with respect to position title(s), organization/employer, dates, location(s), etc.
- Provide a brief description of primary responsibilities.
- Be concise and start points using strong, action-oriented verbs in your description; quantify success where possible.
- Provide details with respect to accomplishments and related skills.
- If professional experiences go back 10 to 15 years, you may want to list only title(s), organization(s), dates, and location(s); you may want to hold off on including a description and additional details.

Professional Activities/Associations

- Provide details regarding any college, community-related activities or professional associations.
- Include the positions held.
- Describe your specific accomplishments, awards and honors.

- Identify leadership roles.
- List presentations, publications, papers, etc.

Certification and Licenses

Some Top Resume Mistakes

Typos and Grammatical Errors

Your resume is a reflection of you and should be perfect. If it isn't, employers may draw unflattering conclusions about you. The hiring manager may think "if this person doesn't care enough to proofread his/her own resume, how much will they possibly care about our customers? How conscientious can they possibly be?" Proofread, and then proofread again. Then share it with several other people for their review.

Lack of Focus or Too General an Objective

Having a sharp focus is extremely important – an employer or hiring manager may quickly glance at or even take as little as 10 to 20 seconds to review a resume. Your resume should share what you want to do and what you are good at – showing a clear match between yourself as the applicant and the particular job's requirements. In addition, a specific objective is always better than a vague or general one. Provide a specific objective that focuses on the employers needs as well as your own. Write a clearly defined career objective – one that conveys the experience, skills and training that best serve your overall professional goals.

Don't Stretch the Truth

If you've caught the attention of a hiring manager and have become a serious candidate, they will most likely be trying to verify the facts on your resume. If you've gotten an offer, there may be a chance that the employer may hire an outside firm to do a background check. Avoid the headaches and embarrassment of 'stretching the truth' – tell the truth in the first place.

The "One Size Fits All" Resume Style

A successful resume is one that is tailored to the job you are trying to get. Write a resume specifically for the targeted employer and position. Clearly show how and why you fit the position in a specific organization.

Lack of Specifics or Focusing Too Strongly on Duties Instead of Accomplishments

Employers need to understand what you've done and accomplished; and therefore, your resume should consist of high-impact accomplishments that sell your qualifications – avoid simply listing job duties and responsibilities on your resume. Provide details on what you have accomplished in your various activities; then go beyond by showing what was required and demonstrate how you made a difference. Focus on the details and specifics needed to catch the employer's attention and how they set you apart from other candidates.

A Resume that is Too Short or Too Long

There is no hard and fast rule as to the appropriate length of a resume. In general, it should be long enough to attract a hiring manager to contact you. Strive to keep your resume concise and focused on your key selling points. Consider a one-page resume if you have fewer than 10 years of experience, are considering a career change and your experience isn't necessarily relevant, and you've held one or two positions with one employer. Consider a two-page resume if you have had 10 or more years of experience or if your field requires technical or engineering skills or you need the space to provide the details of your technical experience. Consider a resume that is two pages or longer if you have a lengthy career or lengthy record of leadership accomplishments or in an academic or scientific field with an extensive list of publications, speaking engagements, professional courses, licenses or patents.

Don't go on about irrelevant or redundant experiences. But, don't cut yourself short eliminating relevant details or notable achievements by trying to conform to one-page.

Weak or Lack of Action Verbs

Let your actions jump off the page and catch a hiring manager's attention. Avoid dull or out-of-date words or phrases like "was responsible for," "provided" or "assisted with." Use strong action-oriented verbs, such as "resolved," "developed," "steered" or "influenced." Active verbs can inspire an employer or hiring manger to contact you.

Leaving off Important Information

Try not to eliminate mentioning of "extra" jobs you may have taken to earn money while in school. The skills and experiences gained may be more important than you think. In addition, don't bury key skills in listings at the bottom of your resume if they are relevant to your field or are key to the position you are applying for.

Visually Too Busy

Is your resume visually attractive? Does it appear disorganized? Does it appear too wordy? Show your resume to several other professionals to obtain their opinion.

Incorrect Contact Information

Always double check your contact information. If an employer can't contact you with the information you have provided, they may not attempt to contact you at all.

Preparing and Sending Electronic Versions of Your Resume

More than ever employers are using online applications and tracking systems for employment. This means making sure that your resume is easy to upload onto a web-based system and easy to download for the employer. Keep the following in mind when preparing your resume for electronic use:

- If you are able, convert your resume to PDF format. This will secure the layout and formatting that you used when preparing your resume.
- If you are unable to convert your resume to PDF format, make sure you limit special formatting, using universally accepted fonts and avoiding special characters or graphics. In addition, turn off any "track changes" editing functions that may have been used when preparing your resume.
- Use appropriate file names with clear identification.
- Use a professional email address.
- Avoid 'misdirected' resumes — take the time to learn who the correct contact is or who is responsible for hiring in the department you are targeting.

Cover Letter

When preparing and forwarding your resume, you should always include a cover letter. The cover letter that you write may play a large part in how effective the response to your resume will be. A good letter may make the difference between getting a job interview and having your application ignored.

The cover letter is a chance to sell yourself to a potential employer and can be just as important as your resume. It, however, serves as a separate function — it should complement your resume, not duplicate it.

Your cover letter is about what you can do for the employer and should:

- Be an introduction of yourself and your reason for writing – share with them that you are interested in the company and want to fill a need that they have.
- Be an opportunity to sell yourself – briefly highlight previously held skills or positions that may be applicable to the position you are seeking; share any additional experiences and competencies that you feel may be important to the employer and how they may benefit the company.
- Provide an opening for next steps – close the letter by indicating what you would like to happen next. Tell them where you can be reached and indicate that you will follow up with them in a few days, that you will follow up with a phone call to make sure that your information has been received and to arrange an interview. Be assertive, but polite.

Other writing tips:

- Personalize your letter – when possible, address your cover letter to the individual responsible for filling the position. Avoid addressing a letter as "To whom it may concern."
- Keep your letter clear and concise – your cover letter should be interesting enough to get the reader's attention, but should be only an introduction to your resume, not a repeat of it.
- Avoid clichés – be unique; don't let your letter read like everyone else's.
- Be positive and confident.
- Be polite and professional.
- Be compelling, personable and brief – you have a very short period of time to convince the

employer to invite you to meet with them.

- Be available – clearly state how you can be reached and when you would be available for further discussion.
- Use correct grammar, spelling and punctuation and be sure to proofread! Typos and grammatical errors say a lot about the kind of work you do and can suggest that you may not care.
- Thank the employer for his/her time.

Visit the following websites for examples of resumes and cover letters:

- http://jobsearch.about.com/od/sampleresumes/a/sampleresumes.htm;
- http://www.resume-resource.com/online.html

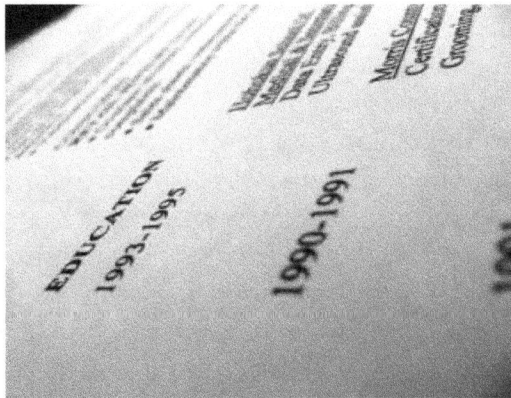

4

Interviewing Basics

Interviewing is one of the most important elements in the job search process. It can, however, be one of the most stressful – even for those who have gone on many. Interviewing can be a skill that improves and becomes easier with preparation and practice.

Some may consider the job interview "a conversation with a purpose." Your goal at the interview is to show the employer or hiring manager that you have the skills, background and ability necessary to do the job and that you fit into the organization and its culture. Preparing for and being part of the interview process also provides the opportunity for you to gather information about the job, the organization, and future opportunities to determine if the position and environment meet your objectives and goals.

You've secured that interview, now it's time to share with the interviewer why you are there.

Prepare in advance. Preparing for an interview can be the single-most effective thing you can do to enhance the likelihood of success in getting a job. It will improve your ability to answer interview questions appropriately, confidently, and help you to make a good impression.

It pays to be well prepared for your interview. Some basic interviewing tips include (but are not limited to):

Preparation:

- Research the company – the more you know about the company and the position you are applying for, the better you will do.
- Have a specific job or jobs in mind.
- Review your qualifications for the job.
- Be ready to briefly describe your experience, showing how it relates it the job.
- Be ready to answer broad questions, such as "Why should I hire you?" "Why do you want this job?" "What are your strengths and weaknesses?"
- Have extra copies of your resume available to take to the interview.
- Practice an interview with a friend or relative.

Personal appearance:

- Be well groomed; make sure your hair is neat and your nails clean; avoid heavy perfume or cologne.
- Prepare yourself the night before with a good night's sleep allowing yourself to be well rested.
- Dress appropriately. Find out what is appropriate for your industry and the company. Also make sure your clothes are clean and pressed and your shoes are polished.

The interview:

- Arrive early.
- Learn the name of your interviewer and greet him or her with a firm handshake.
- Use good manners with everyone you meet.
- Make a good impression – you only have a few seconds to make a good first impression which can influence the rest of the interview and even determine whether you get the job.
- Relax and answer each question concisely.
- Use proper English – avoid slang.
- Be cooperative and enthusiastic.
- Use body language to show interest – make eye contact and look attentive.
- Ask questions about the position and the organization, but avoid questions whose answers can easily be found on the company website.
- Also avoid asking questions about salary and benefits unless a job offer is made.
- Thank the interviewer when you leave; and shake hands.
- Send a short thank you note following the interview. Be simple and brief with your thank you; express your appreciation for the interviewer's

time; show enthusiasm for the job; and get across that you want the job and can do it.

Information to bring to an interview:

- Social Security card.
- Government-issued identification (driver's license).
- Resume and/or application; have extra copies available.
- References. Employers sometimes require three references. Get permission before using anyone as a reference. Make sure that they will give you a good reference. Try to avoid using relatives as references.
- Transcripts. Some employers may require an official copy of transcripts to verify grades, coursework, dates of attendance, and highest grade completed or degree awarded.

The following is a basic guideline to some of the types of interviews conducted.

Informational Interview

An Informational Interview is a meeting designed to help you collect career and industry advice. It is not a job interview but rather an interview with an individual working in your field of interest to gain an understanding of the field or to seek additional information about a specific type of job, about a career direction or to gain invaluable, up-do-date knowledge about a specific business, industry or company.

Benefits of Informational Interviews:

- They allow you to gather valuable firsthand information from industry professionals on career planning and job search strategies.
- You have an opportunity to obtain the "insiders" point of view and discover the "realities" of a particular career field and what is it may be like to work in a given industry; they can validate or dismiss what was previously heard or assumed about a particular line of work or organization.
- They can help you to determine whether the career path you have chosen is compatible with your skills, interests, lifestyle and goals.
- They allow you to obtain suggestions on how and where to acquire the experience and knowledge required.
- They assist with your gaining interview experience and developing confidence in interviewing with professionals by discussing your interests and goals.
- They help you to gain access to the hidden job market through networking and help you to expand your network of contacts in your field of interest for future opportunities and gaining referrals to other professionals in your area of interest.

The subject areas that can be discussed during an informational interview include: the work environment, skill sets or qualifications, industry trends, career paths, typical compensation, challenges or rewards, and career growth.

Preparation is the key to success – you should prepare as you would for a Standard (or Traditional) interview:

- Research the industry or career area of interest and the organization in which the person you are interviewing is affiliated.
- Research the company/organization – review their website, annual reports, marketing information, journals, etc.
- Know your own interests, skills, values and how they relate to the career field represented by the person you are interviewing.
- Prepare a brief profile of who you are and your interest in the field.
- Develop a number of well thought out, open-ended questions.
- If you meet face-to-face, dress appropriately. You want to give a good first impression and look like someone who could be an asset to the profession.

The Informational Interview can be a powerful tool for individuals who are not sure about their career goals or if they feel they lack relevant experience or knowledge about a career position they are looking toward. It is useful for students, those looking for their first job or those considering a transition to a different career.

When meeting someone for an Informational Interview, keep in mind that the person being interviewed is doing you a favor. In addition to being prepared, it is important for you to follow some basic etiquette guidelines:

- Remain professional and keep in mind that this is an important part of your job search.

- Be prepared with research about the industry and the individual.
- Arrange convenient meeting places and times. Be mindful of their schedule and offer to terminate the meeting based on the time originally allocated.
- Have business cards available.
- Dress appropriately.
- Arrive promptly.
- Ask well-prepared and informed questions; take brief notes as appropriate.
- Offer to pay any bills associated with the meeting.
- A follow up thank you note is not only appropriate, but recommended.
- Keep in mind that it is inappropriate to ask for a job during an Informational Interview.

Standard (Traditional) Interview

The Standard (or Traditional) Interview is a formal meeting and discussion, usually in person, arranged between you and an employer or hiring manager for the purposes of exchanging information. This type of interview uses broad-based questions that will allow the employer to evaluate whether you have the skills and abilities necessary to perform the job, whether you possess the enthusiasm and work ethic expected, and whether you fit into the organization.

Behavior-based Interview

A Behavior-based Interview is a structured interview process where candidates are asked to describe specific situations that focus on job related experience, behavior, knowledge, skills and abilities. Employers are looking to see how a candidate's past behavior and performance may be relative to or predict their future performance and behavior. It allows an employer to see patterns that may be missed with basic questions.

The interviewer is listening for specific examples of how you have handled situations or problems in the past as these may be similar to situations that may arise for their company. This allows a candidate to talk about their accomplishments and how they have succeeded in certain areas of interest.

When preparing for a Behavior-based Interview review some of your personal stories prior to the interview. Determine what success stories may apply to the position you are seeking. This will enable you to have examples in mind and will not catch you off guard.

- Assess the type of position you are applying for; try to obtain the job description and skills required for the position.
- Review your background – what skills do you possess? How do they relate to the job objective?
- Identify examples of your experience where you can demonstrate the skills required and 'prepare a story' about your use of the particular skill or knowledge.
- If possible, quantify results.
- Be prepared to provide examples about results that did not turn out well or as you had planned. What did you do when this happened? What was the result?

5

Excelling at the Job Interview

You've secured the interview; now it's time to share with the interviewer everything you have to offer. There are plenty of ways you can promote yourself and get one step closer to the job offer. Make these steps positive and successful ones by emphasizing the experiences in your background that best fit what the interviewer is looking for.

We previously discussed the importance of preparing for your interview and how this can be the difference between success and failure. Interviewers are looking for a reason to hire you – now is your opportunity to rise to the occasion.

We have provided additional details for your preparation and for you to keep in mind when planning for an interview, whether Informational, Standard (Traditional) or Behavior-based:

- Do your homework – research the company before the interview and obtain as much as possible about its services, products, customers and competition. This will give you an edge in understanding and addressing the company's needs.
  - ☐ Review the organization's website.
  - ☐ Obtain and review annual reports, sales brochures, marketing information, on-line journals, etc.
  - ☐ If possible, speak with others who work in the organization or who are in similar positions.

- Assess your skills and abilities and determine whether your interests, experience, skills and goals match the job you are seeking. Assess the goals and values of the organization; are they in alignment with yours? Assess your strengths and weaknesses.

- Update your resume
  - ☐ Make sure you're using the appropriate format – does your resume highlight your accomplishments and compliment your career path?
  - ☐ Is your resume free of grammatical and spelling errors? Is it free of typos? Is it visually appealing?

- Practice good nonverbal communication – you are looking to demonstrate confidence.

- Find out the logistics of the interview
  - ☐ When is the interview scheduled for?
  - ☐ Who will be interviewing you?
    - ☐ Find out the name and job title of the interviewer; see if you can review their business profile.
    - ☐ One-on-one or Panel?
  - ☐ How long will the interview likely be? Will there be subsequent interviews?
  - ☐ Will you be shown around the organization?
  - ☐ Will there be a test?
  - ☐ Will there be further interviews?

- Be prepared and organized with materials you wish to bring with you to the interview.
  - ☐ Bring your resume and other background materials you wish to share during the interview.
  - ☐ Bring a list of questions you may have for the employer.
  - ☐ Bring a pad of paper for note taking.
  - ☐ Get solid references – ask their permission prior to your interview and obtain the best contact information for them. Prepare reference material to have in the event they are requested.
  - ☐ Bring other necessary materials or documentation which may include your passport, driver's license, or social security card.

- Practice interview questions and answers.
  - ☐ Practice your answers to assure confidence.
  - ☐ Consider videotaping a practice interview.
  - ☐ Preparing your responses to interview questions in advance will help you to stay relaxed.

- Dress for the Interview – it is important to know what to wear to an interview and to be well-groomed.
  - ☐ Find out what clothing is appropriate for your industry or for the company before the interview. It is better to dress too conservatively than too casually.
  - ☐ Always maintain a professional appearance, and dress for confidence.

- Be prompt and professional
  - ☐ Always arrive early.
  - ☐ Obtain proper directions to the interview in advance, leaving extra time for traffic, parking, or other events that may occur.
  - ☐ If you are running late, contact the employer immediately.
  - ☐ Be pleasant to everyone you meet when you arrive at your interview.
  - ☐ Turn your cell phone off.

- Sell Yourself
  - ☐ Develop your 'elevator speech' – your strengths, experience, and what sets you apart from other candidates.

- Be sure to send a follow up the interview with a note thanking the interviewer for their time and consideration and reiterating your interest in the position.

Some additional areas to focus on or ways to enhance the basics of interviewing so that you can further excel at your interview may include (but are not limited to):

Be the Solution

Prepare for an interview by identifying problems that may exist and which require a position to be filled. Prepare examples of how you can solve those problems and share how you've solved similar problems in the past by telling stories and providing specific results achieved.

Be Specific

Be prepared with specifics about your skills and achievements providing relevant details. For example, talk about teams you've worked with and what you've learned from them rather than just indicating that you "work well with others." If you want to share with someone how "detail oriented" you are, prepare a story about your attention to detail that had an impact.

Quantify Your Achievements

What are my greatest achievements and how do they set me apart from other candidates? Be succinct and direct when highlighting these successes.

Prepare to Talk About your Resume

Your resume forms an outline for part of the interview. Use the interview to elaborate on or explain the information provided by talking "how" you succeeded, your accomplishments, skills you've gained, and any praise given.

Be Aware of your Nonverbal Communication

Be aware of your posture and facial expressions. Sit or stand up straight, make eye contact and connect with a good, firm handshake. The first nonverbal impression can be a great beginning to your interview, but could be a quick ending to it as well.

Be Positive

Avoid complaints about previous employment or employers. Complaining will likely make you seem difficult to work with.

Be Honest

Lying about your degree, qualification or experience will come back to haunt you.

Listen

From the beginning of the interview, the interviewer is providing information either directly or indirectly. If you are not hearing it, you are missing an opportunity. Good communication skills include listening and letting the person know you have heard what has been said.

Don't Talk Too Much

When you have not prepared ahead of time, you risk the mistake of rambling when answering interview questions. Telling the interviewer more than is necessary can be a mistake. Avoid personal details. Be concise.

Don't Get Too Comfortable

An interview is a professional meeting. Bring energy and enthusiasm to an interview but don't make the meeting about making friends.

Use Appropriate Language and Avoid Controversial Topics

Use professional language and avoid inappropriate words or references (to age, race, religion, etc.). Religion, politics and controversial topics are off limits.

Attitude Can Play a Key Role

Find the right balance between confidence, professionalism and modesty.

Answer the Question

If an interviewer asks for an example or asks a question designed to prompt a sample of past behavior and you fail to relate a specific question or example you may miss an opportunity to prove your ability or skills. If you are unclear or if you feel you misunderstood a question being asked, get further clarification.

Ask Questions

Part of knowing how to interview is being ready to ask questions and demonstrating an interest in the company. It also gives you an opportunity to find out if the position and company values meet your objectives. The best questions come from listening during the interview and asking for additional information or clarification.

Don't Appear Desperate

Remain calm, cool and confident. Help the interviewer to believe in you.

At your interview the questions asked can range from questions about your work history, questions about you, questions about the job and the company, and questions about how you look at your future. Here are a few sample interview questions. How would you respond if you were asked these questions?

Questions: Why do you want this job?

The employer is looking to see that you can demonstrate your research of the employer or organization and that you are able tie your knowledge of them into the skills that led you to apply. You want to share with them that your interest in the job or organization is beneficial to the employer and includes a career fit, cultural fit, interest in their business, personal fit and your ability to be successful at the job.

Question: How do you handle conflict?

An interviewer wants to know how you react to conflict and how you might manage it. Focus your answer on the process that you would use to resolve the conflict. Don't focus on difficulty with a previous boss or co-worker, for example. Instead, highlight your interpersonal skills, maturity and ability to stay calm in the face of difficulty. Emphasize techniques you might use to diffuse the conflict, such as determining the other person's position, finding out the cause of the conflict, not conveying blame and not becoming emotional. Demonstrate your ability to work together to reach an acceptable resolution.

Question: Describe a situation in which you lead a team.

Graduate positions sometime involve people management where one is expected to plan, organize and guide the work of others as well as motivate them. The interviewer need to assess how well you relate to other people, the role you take in a group and whether you are able to focus on goals and targets. Outline a situation, your role and the overall task. Describe any problems that arose and how they were resolved. Describe the result and how you learned from it.

Question: What has been a difficult situation you have had to face?

An interviewer is trying to determine what your definition of difficult is and how you might approach challenges and problems. Focus on a situation that you feel most people might consider difficult. Think of a specific situation that you may have had and how it tested your skills and abilities; determine a positive outcome. Highlight the way you analyzed the situation, the skills you used to deal with it, and what your contribution to resolving the issue was. Always end on a positive note. Some examples of difficult situations may include disciplining an employee, unreasonable goals and deadlines, unreasonable customers or clients, or facing an unethical work situation.

Question: Where would you like to be in your career five years from now?

The interviewer is trying to get a sense of your personal goals, ambition, drive and direction. They will be looking for responses relevant to their needs. You will need to determine how much you want to share. If you want to own your own business five years from now and need experience in a competitive company, don't share this. However, if your career goals include becoming a vice president in that time frame and are interviewing in a merit-based environment, you may want to share this with the interviewer.

Question: Tell me about your proudest achievement (or accomplishment).

This is a behavioral question so you will want to share a specific example from your professional experiences and show evidence of skills relevant to the job (communication, initiative, teamwork, determination). Select an example or story about how you handled a project that is significant to you and provide details discussing the situation, your role and what you did, any process you set up and any obstacles you had to overcome.

Question: Give me an example of a time when you had to think out of the box.

The interviewer is asking about your innovativeness, creativity, and initiative and looking not only about a specific idea but how you came up with it and what you did with it. This is a behavior question that should be relevant to the job you are interviewing for. Consider how you may have solved a customer's problem, or how you may have improved an internal process.

Question: What can you offer us that other candidates cannot?

The interviewer is asking "Why should we hire you?" They are asking you to compare yourself to other candidates; tell them why you are special. Your response to this question should sum up your main selling points keeping in mind that you want to relate your answer specifically to the job requirements. Consider past experiences that are related to the job, your specialized knowledge, relevant growth or change, skills, future potential, etc.

Question: Tell me about a time you faced an ethical dilemma.

The interviewer is looking for a discussion regarding your ethical standards and honesty. You may want to think back to some areas when you may have been tested in the past. Describe the situation and how you dealt with it; share with the interviewer how you didn't "blow the whistle" on a fellow employee but how you may have taken care of the problem yourself.

116

Question: Tell me about a time when you failed.

The interviewer is looking to discuss what you may have learned from a situation that went awry and how you may have had to handle any resulting fallout. Failure can come in many forms – taking the wrong action, omission, or not doing enough or taking action soon enough. Describe a situation where you learned something substantive and share how you learned from the mistake.

Question: Tell me about a project you worked on that required heavy analytical thinking.

The interviewer is looking for you to demonstrate your competency by asking you how you used your analytical skills to achieve a goal. What formal and informal analysis did you do? How did you structure the project? What obstacles did you face and how did you overcome them?

Question: Why do you want to leave your current position?

The interviewer is interested in your long-term commitment and whether you would be satisfied in your new position. Prepare a response that is positive and that you are comfortable with. Refer to overall fit, personality or new directions. Discuss your goals and readiness for a new role carefully emphasizing benefits to the employer and not your personal goals.

Question: Tell me about yourself.

The interviewer is interested in seeing how you present yourself but is not looking for details from your resume. This question typically occurs at the beginning of the interview and is geared toward your sharing who you are professionally and why you are there. Try to connect your background, knowledge and interests with the job you are interviewing for. This will make your response more compelling. Leave personal details out.

Question: How would you describe your work style?

The interviewer is interested in hearing how you understand and articulate your work. There may be a requirement for someone highly organized or there may be a specific way in which the team you would join might work; the interviewer is interested in whether you would fit. You will need to think about how you work and in what type of environments you work well. Are you highly structured? Do you focus on one thing at a time or can you work on multiple projects simultaneously? Do you work better with structure or thrive in chaos? When answering, be specific and back up your answer with brief examples.

Question: What is your management style?

This is a question for management-level candidates where the interviewer is looking to find out if your management style fits, if you have the management ability and how much you understand your own work style.

Discuss how you lead and develop a team, your communication skills, how you organize and plan, and how you execute, manage and measure progress.

Question: How would your past experience translate into success in this job?

The interviewer is asking you to effectively communicate your experiences and their connection with the job. You will need to share with them clearly why you have what it takes to do the job well. You might begin with reviewing some of the top requirements of the position and sharing how you meet or exceed them. You might share your background and how it has prepared you for this job.

Question: What are your weaknesses?

Choose and describe a weakness that would not negatively affect your ability to do the job, one that you have worked on or are working on to improve; describe the action(s) you have taken or are taking.

Question: What are your strengths?

Consider the requirements of the job and compare these with your skills, abilities and experience. You want to consider how you can match these as these should be your major strengths.

Other sample interview questions include:

What influenced you to study the course you did?

What are the skills and attributes that make a good ...? (chemist, technical analyst, for example)

The job requires a passion for "hands on" lab work. What laboratory techniques are you familiar with? What makes you a good technician in the lab?

Can you give me an example of when you used your initiative to solve a problem?

What motivates you? Describe a situation in which you motivated others.

Describe a situation where you had to deal with a difficult person. What was the situation? How did you handle it?

How do you organize your time and plan activities?

This job requires the ability to work autonomously. Do you think you can do that?

Tell me about fieldwork you have done.

Just as the initial contact with your interviewer (and other employees) provides a powerful initial impression, the close at the end should be strong as it can also offer lasting impressions. You will be asked whether you have any other questions. Ask any relevant question that has not yet been addressed. Highlight any of your strengths that have not been discussed. If another interview is to be scheduled, obtain the necessary details. If this is a final interview, find out when the decision is to be made and when you may follow up.

Thank the person(s) at the conclusion of the interview, but also follow up with a thank you note to all of the participants at the interview(s). Thank them for their time and consideration while restating your interest in the position and reminding them of the valuable traits you can bring to the job and the company.

Let your references know that they are going to be contacted. Allow them time to prepare for and expect the call. Let them know how important it is that they take the call and provide you with a reference.

6

Working With a Search Firm

For many individuals the job search can be very stressful whether you are looking for your first job or considering a job change. In an unpredictable and highly competitive job market today and with unemployment at an all-time high, making a decision to work with a search firm or recruiter can be a valuable tool and help you to broaden your job search and chances of success.

Consider some of these benefits:

- Search firms have contacts in industries and at companies that you may not have, may not be aware of, or that may not be publicly available. They can provide access to opportunities you may not find anywhere else. They can help you market your resume and provide you with the exposure needed to reach potential employers.

- Only candidates whose qualifications meet the job requirements are referred to the hiring company for consideration; and when coming from a search firm, employers know that you have been screened, meet the client's specifications and you are serious about the position.

- Most good recruiters develop and nurture relationships with their clients over a period of time. These relationships can be invaluable – they have the trust and attention of decision makers who are difficult to reach. They can get you in front of the right people. When represented by a recruiter, they can communicate valuable information to the employer that may not be relayed on your resume, therefore securing an interview that you would not have secured on your own.

- Recruiters have insight into positions, companies, and the interview processes and can assist you in the preparation of an interview. This can enable you to have a better understanding and assessment of how the employer evaluates candidates, what the employer considers important qualities and other criteria they are looking for so that you can highlight these areas in your discussion with them. You can then prepare and focus your efforts on emphasizing your background, skills and experience in a way that best fits the employer's needs.

- Following an interview, a recruiter is in a position to communicate with the company for feedback. This constructive feedback, as well as any that you provide to the recruiter, can help in any needed improvement of your interview skills for future interview opportunities.

- A recruiter can educate you, prepare you, and coach you through all aspects of the interview and hiring process.
- When a company is ready to offer you a position, the recruiter can have a significant role in assisting you with this. They can assist you in negotiating any details related to the offer – i.e., salary, benefits, start date, etc.

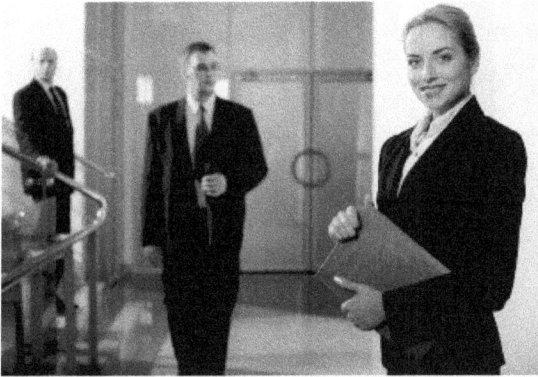

Executive search firms (or head hunters) are firms that are hired and paid by employers to recruit for higher-level jobs. There are two types of executive search firms – retainer and contingency.

Retainer firms are hired by individual employers to recruit for a specific position that is available within their company. They work with high-level professional jobs and are paid a retainer fee for the search even if they

125

are unsuccessful in filling the available position. They usually work with fewer employers than contingency firms.

Contingency firms work for several employers to recruit for various mid-level professional jobs. They are paid a fee if they successfully fill a position.

Executive search firms are useful to job seekers who have the experience that their clients are looking for. These types of search firms typically prefer to work with people who are currently employed; however, they will consider working with individuals who have lost their job through no fault of their own. Contact a search firm that specializes in your industry or area of interest.

There are many search firms out there. Be selective in choosing the firm or recruiter to represent you. This person should make you feel comfortable enough to share all your reasons for the career move. Confidentiality should be of utmost importance. You should get the sense that this person represents client companies that would be of interest to you. Be certain that your resume will not be sent to a prospective opportunity without first discussing the position with you.

If there is mutual interest in working together, you will likely be required to send them a resume and/or schedule a time for an interview. You can expect feedback on your resume. Even if the firm does not have a current opportunity for you, ask for resume input as they see so many, input can be quite valuable.

126

When meeting for an interview with a search firm, conduct yourself in a manner as you would with a prospective employer. Dress for an interview, schedule adequate time for the meeting and ask questions. If you are concerned with the interview process or how to present any aspect of your experience, get the recruiter's input. Part of their role is to help you overcome and present any questionable aspects of your background.

7

Networking

Networking can be defined (see Merriam-Webster) as "the exchange of information or services among individuals, groups, or institutions; or the cultivation of productive business relationships." Our discussion here will be about networking as it relates to your job search. It is a process of connecting with people who might have information about potential job openings or introducing you to others who can provide you with this information. These contacts can be personal relationships, family, or others that you meet in an informal gathering. They can also be business relationships you have developed with customers, supervisors, subordinates, and competitors that you have faced during the course of your career. Also consider other contacts at professional meetings, conferences or conventions; volunteer groups; members of your social clubs or religious groups; former colleagues, for example. The ultimate goal of networking is to meet the person who has the authority to hire you for the job you want.

Networking is about building relationships and getting to know people. Adopting a networking lifestyle of connecting and helping others can help you to find the right job, make valuable connections in your field, and stay focused and motivated during your job search.

Networking can be a valuable tool when searching for a job:

- The job you are looking for may not even be advertised. Networking leads to information and job leads that may not be announced yet. It offers a job pipeline that you may otherwise never know about.
- Employers are inundated with resumes and rely on referrals as a way to obtain good candidates. Some employers prefer to interview and hire people who are referred to them.
- Job listings can draw large numbers of applicants and a great deal of competition. Networking makes you a recommended member of a smaller pool. Anything you can do to stand out against your competitors can help you get the job you want.
- Networking is a two-way street – it should benefit both parties to be effective. Don't ask your network for help only when you are in need – be prepared to return the favor when asked.

- Networking within your groups can help establish strong connections and ultimately help you to learn about and get noticed for great opportunities.
- Your networking contacts can provide you with information about new careers or companies, help you to clarify your goals, provide feedback on your resume, and help you to improve or sharpen your interviewing skills.

Build and Expand Your Network

- Visit or join professional or trade associations in your field or area of interest. Get involved with civic, social or religious organizations. Attend meetings or events with people in your field or area of interest. Many members wish to help job seekers and often know employers with available positions.
- Find a mentor who has experience in your field or area of interest. Get their advice and use them as a sounding board.
- Talk with your friends, family, professors, former supervisor or manager. Practice selling yourself to those you know.
- Follow through with referrals or leads. After your initial networking and research, you will want to meet with these contacts, introduce yourself and obtain more information or job leads. You may be able to set a meeting for an informational interview or arrange additional communications by phone or by mail.
- Have business cards even if you are not currently employed.

Networking Etiquette

- Always look for opportunities to give something back. Be prepared to offer something of value to those who are taking the time to help you.
- When gathering information about your field or about specific opportunities, ask for the information, not for a job.
- Let people know you appreciate their help by sending a thank you note or by letting them know the results of the information they gave you. Offer to help them in return.

Practice Effective Communication

- Keep your contacts informed about your efforts in the job search.
- Send your thank you letter soon after your interview.
- Keep conversations friendly but professional. Provide a brief summary of your objectives and then share your accomplishments and how they relate to your objective.

Be Prepared

- You may be introduced to new contacts – be prepared to communicate your job search objectives, strengths, accomplishments, etc.
- Unexpected opportunities may arise – if possible have business cards and copies of your resume available.

Keep Track of your Networking Efforts

- Keep a record of the contacts you make, results of those contacts and any follow up that is needed.

- Whenever you meet with someone new, exchange business cards.
- Take notes so you will remember pertinent details on who you met with, the relationship, and the value to your job search.

8

Developing Your
Elevator Pitch

An elevator pitch can be described as a "short
summary used to quickly and simply define a
product, service, or organization and its value
proposition" and "that it should be possible to deliver
the summary in the time span of an elevator ride, or
approximately thirty seconds to two minutes."

Whether you are a business owner, looking for a job,
or building your network, you should be equipped with
an elevator pitch. One of the most important things
you can do is talk about yourself or your business in a
concise way. Your elevator pitch comes in handy when
you attend an event, conference, convention, or other

networking opportunity. Your pitch is an invaluable networking tool and becomes one of your first opportunities to make an impact. For the job seeker, it can be extremely helpful at networking events (i.e. job/career fairs) as well as at job interviews; your pitch may sometimes be the basis for or be incorporated into your cover letter or voicemail message when communicating with a recruiter or prospective employer.

You've just met someone at an event and they ask you "What do you do?" Or, you are at an interview with a potential employer and they begin the discussion with "Tell me a little about yourself." Can you, in about one minute:

- Explain yourself, your business, and your goals or passions?
- Tell an appealing story that engages your listener(s) to actually *listen* and conveys your message in a way that your listener(s) *understands* you?
- Communicate your message quickly, clearly, and distinctly to someone who doesn't even know you? Are you prepared to communicate your message easily while inviting them to want to know more?
- Make sure that what you say is *remembered*?

Here are some of tips for preparing your pitch and being able to provide the right words for that impromptu situation.

- Your pitch should be concise and should typically be no more than about a minute long. Keep your pitch short and focused and include only interesting and relevant information.

- Your pitch should be specific – you want to provide yourself an opportunity to sell yourself. Get straight to the point and talk about aspects that the listening party would be interested in. Target your specific audience and address their specific interests and concerns.
- Your pitch should provide your immediate goals – goals that are concrete, defined and realistic.
- Your pitch should provide unique benefits that you and/or your company bring to a business. Show that what you do that is different or better than others.
- You want to use language that everyone can understand. If you use language that a listener won't understand, you will lose the opportunity to engage them. The job seeker should establish that they have strong communication and organizational skills, again, without providing too much unnecessary detail.
- You want to identify your value proposition and be able to explain why you are qualified to see the problem, how you can help solve the problem, and how you provide the solution. You want to be able to summarize key professional strengths and describe yourself as qualified and accomplished. The job seeker should share that they possess the knowledge and skills necessary to solve the problems or needs of the potential employee and provide a reason for them to believe that they can do the job.
- For the job seeker, an elevator pitch should be directed to who they are professionally and be focused on their goals. It should focus on specific qualifications for the job they are seeking and provide evidence that they are qualified for the

specific job they are seeking.

☐ It should begin by describing their profession and the number of years' experience, and

☐ It should describe skills, qualifications, experiences and accomplishments that are relevant and/or unique.

- If you put together different 'versions' of your pitch, they should convey the same basic message. The job seeker should align themself with the position for which they are interviewing, describing why they want to work for the company and why they would be suited for the position.
- Spend time planning, preparing, and practicing your pitch. Practice with friends and ask them to provide feedback. Rehearse it in front of a mirror so that you become comfortable with your pitch.
- Your pitch should engage your audience with the intent of getting to the next step in a process; i.e. a request for a next meeting or additional interview.
- Although you may consider having several 'versions' of your pitch, your pitch should be natural – not necessarily memorized; one that can be pitched smoothly and without hesitation – and enable you to present to various audiences at various times.
- The job seeker should never include negative aspects about a former or current employer.

Be prepared to pitch at all times – you never know when your opportunity will arise. A well-prepared pitch will enable you to gain confidence and deliver your pitch to the right person, in the right way, at the right time.

9

Career and Job Fairs

A career or job fair is a gathering of employers, recruiters and schools to meet with prospective job seekers. These fairs provide an opportunity to find out what jobs are available in the companies or areas of interest for which you would like to work. They provide you the opportunity to gather important information about the participating companies, to inquire about future job openings with those companies for which you would qualify, and to get the contact information of a company representative for future communications and follow up.

Preparing for and Attending a Career or Job Fair

Attending a career or job fair allows you to meet with employers and representatives who can provide information about general career opportunities as well as specific details on available positions. Career and job fairs are also a great opportunity for expanding your network, developing and refining your interview skills, learning industry information, and gathering information about companies.

- Do your research, have a game plan, and explore your options – research and obtain a list of the attending companies identifying in advance who you want to speak with. Obtain as much information as possible about the companies you want to meet with. Look at the opportunity to browse and meet will all of the available companies and contacts.
- Dress professionally – First impressions matter – dress appropriately. Job fairs require the same attention to attire as interviews. You will, however, want to wear comfortable shoes as there will be long lines.
- Bring a supply of resumes and business cards to hand out to the companies and contacts you connect with.
- Prepare your 'elevator pitch' – think about and be prepared to talk about yourself, your strong points, your goals, your knowledge of and interest in the company and where you want to go with that company. Have a focused response which should include some general background, leadership qualities and what you will bring to the organization. Be prepared to discuss your career

goals and objectives, your work experience, skills and abilities with limited time. You may only have a minute or less actual face time with the company representative – make it count.

- Be Confident – You may be nervous; try to appear as though you aren't by being prepared, looking people in the eye when you speak, being secure in your delivery, and limiting or avoiding filler words ("um").
- Be prepared to discuss your leadership roles, volunteer experience, or interests that could demonstrate leadership ability.
- Arrive early allowing yourself time to review the booths (or tables) and locations and, therefore, being able to find your target companies.
- Network – Take advantage of the opportunity to network with fellow job seekers and other professionals in attendance.
- Be assertive, enthusiastic, and show initiative – Shake hands and introduce yourself to recruiters when you reach the table. Smile and project interest in the company and their job opportunities. Maintain professionalism when addressing recruiters or company representatives. Inquire about ways to access future information and/or job opportunities at a company; take initiative and ask what your next steps may be; and follow up with thank notes after meeting with representatives.
- Don't be overwhelmed by the experience; keep a positive attitude and concentrate on the benefits of the experience.

10

Contract and Temporary Employment

Contract or temporary positions are ever increasing in the science and technology industries and can offer benefits to both the individual and company. A contract or temporary employee is a skilled temporary or hourly employee who is employed by an employment agency or staffing company and who is engaged by that business to provide a specific set of skills or services or to work on a particular project for one of their client companies. Contract or temporary employees are employees of the staffing company, not that of the client company. Arrangements for contract or temporary employment are used for various reasons:

to meet increased business demands, to provide skills that are not available in house, and to reduce costs.

With contract or temporary employment, an employer-employee relationship is established in connection with the terms and conditions being communicated verbally or in the form of a written employment contract. The contract outlines the length of employment, the salary and bonuses (if applicable) to be paid, and other benefits to the employee. The contract also outlines the specific role the employee will play.

- Contract or temporary employees are generally engaged for a set term. There may be provisions in the employment contract that allow for a renewal of the term. A term can typically be associated with the particular project or for a set number of days, months, or years. In the case of a verbal agreement, the assignment may be indefinite in length.
- The amount and manner in which the employee is paid is established. Provisions may be included for an increase based on progress of the project.

Advantages of Contract or Temporary Work

- Employees are paid by the hours of work and may have an opportunity for an 'increased salary' and overtime pay.
- This type of temporary or hourly work offers flexible work options. Candidates can decide the time, place, and how they want to work.
- Contract or temporary work allows you to change your job regularly, particularly if you are working with short-term contracts.

144

- Temporary jobs can give an employee experience in industries or careers they may not have otherwise had an opportunity to try and without the long-term commitment.
- Temporary work can allow you to earn money while you are between jobs or conducting a search for employment.
- Temporary jobs can provide a way to obtain and develop skills and experience while transitioning to your 'ideal' position.
- Treat your temporary job as a "long-term interview." Although the position may begin as temporary, it can provide a foot in the door and an opportunity to join a company you may be interested in working for. It can provide you an opportunity to prove your skill levels and your fit within the culture leading to being hired directly with the company.
- Temporary or contract work may allow you to become aware of a position prior to it being posted outside the company.
- In some instances temporary agencies provide benefits to their workers. Temporary employees who work through an agency may receive paid benefits such as holiday, vacation time, medical and dental coverage, life insurance and a 401K plan. They are an employee of the agency, not the employee of the company where they are placed.

But What About the Independent Contractor?

We've discussed working as a contract or temporary employee, what it means and its possible benefits. You may now ask yourself the question: How does working as an independent contractor compare?

An independent contractor may be defined as a "... person, business, or corporation that provides goods or services to another entity under terms specified in a contract or within a verbal agreement. Unlike an employee, an independent contractor does not work regularly for an employer but works as and when required. Independent contractors are usually paid on a freelance basis. Contractors often work through a limited company or franchise, which they themselves own, or may work through an umbrella company."

146

Generally speaking, an independent contractor provides services to another individual or business, is a separate business entity and is not considered an employee, and maintains control over their schedule and number of hours worked, jobs accepted, and performance of their job. In addition, they may have an investment in equipment, furnish all their own supplies, provide their own insurance, repairs, and all other expenses related to their business. They may also perform a special service that is not in the normal course of business of the employer. This contrasts with the situation for regular employees, who usually work at the schedule required by the employer and whose performance is directly supervised by the employer.

Some independent contractors may work for a number of different organizations throughout the year; however, there are also many independent contractors who work for the same organization for the entire year.

From the IRS's standpoint, they describe the independent contractor as:

People such as doctors, dentists, veterinarians, lawyers, accountants, contractors, subcontractors, public stenographers, or auctioneers who are in an independent trade, business, or profession in which they offer their services to the general public are generally independent contractors. However, whether these people are independent contractors or employees depends on the facts in each case. The general rule is that an individual is an independent contractor if the payer has the right to control or direct only the result of the work and not what will be done and how it will be done. The earnings of a person who is working as an independent contractor are subject to Self-Employment Tax.

If you are an independent contractor, you are self-employed. To find out what your tax obligations are, visit the Self-Employed Tax Center.

You are not an independent contractor if you perform services that can be controlled by an employer (what will be done and how it will be done). This applies even if you are given freedom of action. What matters is that the employer has the legal right to control the details of how the services are performed.

If an employer-employee relationship exists (regardless of what the relationship is called), you are not an independent contractor and your earnings are generally not subject to Self-Employment Tax.

However, your earnings as an employee may be subject to FICA (Social Security tax and Medicare) and income tax withholding.

11

Social Media and Social Networking

We discussed earlier how networking can be an extremely important element in your job search. Social networking is an ideal way to build relationships and can help you to better search for and reach your target job. The relationships you build with social networking can lead you to unadvertised job openings, help you to gain knowledge and understanding of your industry or area of interest, and even lead you to a referral to a company for which you'd like to work.

Social media includes various online tools that enable people to communicate via the Internet to share information and resources; some of these sites include: LinkedIn, Twitter, Facebook. Many people also use their blog, or blogging. While using social media you can promote yourself, get in front of recruiters or potential clients, and connect with people who may be in a position to hire or know someone who does. The following are brief discussions of some of social media tools.

LinkedIn

LinkedIn can be described as a business-related social networking site that allows users to maintain contact details of people with whom they have some level of relationship (the relationships established are called "connections"). Users can invite anyone (whether they are a site user or not) to become a connection. As a professional networking site it allows members to upload their profile and connect and interact with others in their industry or field, participate in groups, and provide answers to questions posted by other members. The types of connections one makes can be useful in many ways:

- LinkedIn is very popular with employers and recruiters – they often post jobs on LinkedIn and search social media for potential candidates.
- LinkedIn allows users to research companies with which they may be interested in working. When searching the name of a given company, one can obtain information about the company ranging from the location of the company's headquarters, what they are about, titles/positions held within the company, and even listings of present and former employees.

- Users can follow different companies and get notification about the new people joining and offers available. They can save (or bookmark) jobs which they may be interested in or for which they would like to apply.
- Job seekers can use LinkedIn to find jobs, people and business opportunities recommended by someone in their contact network; they may be able to obtain an introduction to a potential employer made through a mutual contact.
- Job seekers can increase their visibility on LinkedIn by participating in groups and answering questions on the "Answers" section.
- Recent features allow companies to include an "Apply with LinkedIn" button on job listing pages that allow potential employees to apply for positions using their LinkedIn profiles as resumes.

Twitter

Twitter can be described as a social networking and microblogging (users exchange small elements of content, such as short sentences) service that enables its users to send and read text-based messages or posts (known as tweets). These are text-based posts displayed on the author's profile page and delivered to the author's subscribers who are known as followers. Tweets are publicly visible by default; however, senders can restrict delivery of messages to just their followers.

Twitter describes itself as "a service for friends, family, and co-workers to communicate and stay connected through the exchange of quick, frequent answers to one simple question: What are you doing?"

Similar to LinkedIn, Twitter provides opportunities for the types of connections its users can make:

- A job seeker can increase their visibility by participating in discussions on topics they are well versed in. This can position the job seeker as a knowledgeable professional. Recruiters use Twitter to look for candidates by searching for keywords in their bios.
- Users can be connected to people based on common interests.
- Job seekers are able to follow the companies they are interested in and can keep up with their news or updates; many companies post jobs on Twitter.
- Job seekers can learn about available jobs and connect with those who know about jobs that they would not otherwise know about.
- Job seekers can follow relevant recruiters and people working in your industry.
- Job seekers can follow the brands and businesses that they have an interest in working for. They can look for HR specific handles that are used to announce job openings.

Facebook

Facebook can be described as a social networking service and website that allows a user to create a personal profile, add other users as friends, and exchange messages and information. Facebook allows users to stay in touch with friends, relatives and other acquaintances wherever they are as long as they have access to the Internet. It can bring together people allowing users to join common interest user groups, organized by workplace, school or college.

Once a user has become a member they can identify with people in a group who they want to friend. Group members may likely be open to friending a user because they already have the group in common. This can enable a user to grow their network and obtain information about job opportunities.

Recruiters use Facebook to post jobs and relevant employment information. Be sure to "like" the Facebook pages so that you can receive updated information from companies, resources, and networking contacts.

Blogs

A Blog can be described as a journal published on the web consisting of entries (posts) typically displayed in reverse chronological order with the most recent post appearing first. Blogs are usually maintained by an individual or a small group, are based on a particular subject, and have regular entries. It combines text, images, and links to other blogs, web pages or other media related to the topic. Blogs are typically interactive allowing visitors to leave comments and messages. The interactivity is important and distinguishes blogs from other social media sites.

As a form of social networking, bloggers produce content to post while building social relationships with their readers and other bloggers.

Among the many types of blogs, there are those that are corporate and organizational, both of which can be important to a job seeker when researching companies and areas of interest. Corporate blogs can be used internally to enhance communication and culture in an organization or externally for marketing, branding or public relations. Organizational blogs for clubs and societies are typically used to inform members and interested parties of club or member activities.

Tips for Successful Networking with Social Media

- Maximize your presence online and represent yourself in a positive light. When using social media for a job search, remove anything that you don't want an employer to see. Be mindful of your use of language and any documentation of events that may be inappropriate.
- Focus on building mutually beneficial relationships – don't just connect with people that can help you – think about how you can help them as well. Refer your social media contacts to others; they will reciprocate.
- Join groups that are in your area of interest or discipline and focus on groups or sites that have relevant conversations on your area of expertise. Employers are in these same communities and will have an opportunity to see what you have to offer.
- Create your network and use your groups and communities to share your situation providing them with the type of job you are looking for and the companies you would like to work for.
- Use your research opportunities to follow companies you would like to work for. Observe them and follow their news and updates.
- Dedicate a portion of your day to maintaining your online presence, following new people, or

thanking people for sharing important information. Use this time to keep up with changes to the site functionality and features offered.

In addition:

- Be clear on what you want – Candidates searching for a job need to have a clear focus on what they are looking for in a position. Clearly define what you want and what you can do, and ask your network to actively help you.
- Build and develop a personal and professional online brand that reflects your skills, background, passions, experience and personality. Have a strong, clear and consistent presence across all networks – this helps recruiters get to know you and sets you apart from a list of names and resumes. Update your profile regularly reflecting any appropriate changes.
- Create the connections you need to get the job. Don't just use the connections you already have. Determine who you need to know to land a job and make the connection.
- Protect yourself and keep your profiles private. Only accept Facebook friend requests from people you know. Keep your LinkedIn profile public but choose to only publish certain aspects.
- Engage people in conversation, compliment them on their work, ask questions and acknowledge their expertise – they will be more likely to respond.
- Whether on LinkedIn, Twitter or Facebook, let your friends and followers know that you are looking for a job, and, again, be clear of what type of job you are looking for. If they know you are

available, they will think of you if they hear about an open position.

- Find information out about hiring managers. Look up the hiring manager on LinkedIn and Twitter and learn how you can tailor your communications to meet their needs.
- Develop a hyperlink (or URL) to your resume. Add this URL to Twitter and your LinkedIn profile. This offers employers another way of getting in touch with you and seeing how you interact online.
- Join industry chats on Twitter. Look for chats that revolve around your industry or area of interest. Joining online conversations helps you keep up to date on the industry, meet helpful contacts, and share your expertise. You may also want to network with other job seekers through regular conversations like #jobhuntchat or #careerchat.
- Seek out job search advice. These networks are great places to find advice on job hunting and to socialize with other job seekers. Join LinkedIn groups that focus on job search. Follow career experts on Twitter, and similar pages on Facebook.
- Optimize your LinkedIn profile to let recruiters find you. Come up with three or four keywords that you use to search for your job and include them in your profile. Monitor how often your profile appears in searches and how many people are viewing your profile. Learn about LinkedIn's advanced features – for example, "Advanced Job Search," "Request Referral," "Groups" and "Answers," and "JobsInsider toolbar."
- Search Twitter for job openings. Search by location, job titles, company names or hashtags such as #jobs, #job, #jobsearch, #jobseeker, #career.

Monitor keywords that relate to the jobs that you are applying to as well as words like "opening," "position," etc.

- Learn about Twitter's advanced features – for example, TwitJobSearch, which is a job search engine that collects job listings and posts them.
- Another effective tool may be Google Alerts. Google Alerts are emails that you can receive that provide updates of latest relevant Google results (web, news, etc.). Google Alerts can help you: monitor job leads that don't appear on job boards, find out what is being said about a particular company, and keep up to date on a competitor or industry.
- Review other sites, such as Indeed.com or Simply Hired.com. These sites are employment websites and online recruitment networks that provide search engines for job listings and that aggregate job listings from thousands of websites, including job boards, newspapers, associations, and company career pages. Among some of the services included are: job search, job trends, industry trends, salary search, job competition index, and website forums. Indeed.com also allows job seekers to apply directly to jobs on their site.

12

Tips From a Recruiter

A job search is a job!

Have a clear idea of what you're looking for, why you're looking and your goals. Be able to communicate this. Practice that communication.

Clearly understand your short-term and long-term goals. Are they in alignment?

Network, Network, Network

If you give in a networking situation, you are more likely to receive.

Have a strong resume – customize it to the job you are interviewing for.

Be prepared for an interview – research the company and market; research the position you are interviewing for. With a behavioral-based interview, have specific examples of accomplishments.

Develop your interview skills – use positive language, good eye contact, open body language and enthusiasm; demonstrate interest in the position you are interviewing for.

Practice interviewing and obtain feedback; develop an elevator pitch you can use at career and job fairs.

Have informational meetings/interviews with professionals in your area of interest.

Join professional and industrial associations and organizations.

Smile and keep a positive attitude; be polite and friendly.

Listen and engage. Follow the lead of the interviewer. Don't interrupt; if you don't hear or don't understand a question, ask for clarification.

Be honest – don't exaggerate or misrepresent yourself on your resume or in an interview.

At the close of the interview, be certain that you have addressed all of the company's concerns or questions.

Send follow-up thank you notes to everyone you meet.

Remember a recruiter is not a social worker, not your therapist, and will formulate an opinion of you as any other potential employer will.

A recruiter can be a wealth of information if you are directed, focused and taking your job search seriously.

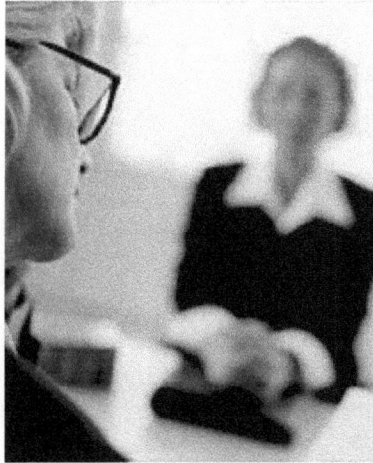

13

Associations and Professional Groups

The following is a listing and brief description of several associations and professional groups providing not only who they are and what they stand for, but also sharing their significance in each of their respective fields The information that follows was obtained through several Internet sites, including the Associations' or Professional Groups' websites.

American Academy of Forensic Sciences (AAFS)

Founded in 1948, and headquartered in Colorado Springs, Colorado, the American Academy of Forensic Sciences (AAFS) is known as the world's most prestigious forensic science organization. The AAFS is a professional association committed to the promotion of education and the advancement of accuracy, precision, and specificity in the forensic sciences. The Academy's membership includes physicians, attorneys, dentists, toxicologists, physical anthropologists, document examiners, digital evidence experts, psychiatrists, physicists, engineers, criminalists, educators, digital evidence experts, and others who actively practice forensic science and, in many cases, also teach and conduct research in the field.

As stated on their website, the mission of the Academy is: "a multi-disciplinary professional organization that provides leadership to advance science and its application to the legal system. The objectives of the Academy are to promote professionalism, integrity, competency, education, foster research, improve practice, and encourage collaboration in the forensic sciences."

For more information about the American Academy of Forensic Sciences (AAFS), visit their website at www. aafs.org.

American Association for the Advancement of Science (AAAS)

Founded in 1848 and considered to be one of the world's largest general scientific societies, the American Association for the Advancement of Science (AAAS) is an international non-profit organization with goals of promoting cooperation among scientists, defending scientific freedom, encouraging scientific responsibility, and supporting scientific education and science outreach by serving as an educator, leader, spokesperson and professional association.

As stated on their website, the mission of the Association is to: "advance science, engineering, and innovation throughout the world for the benefit of all people." The Association also listed the broad goals that they have set as:

- Enhance communication among scientists, engineers, and the public;
- Promote and defend the integrity of science and its use;
- Strengthen support for the science and technology enterprise;
- Provide a voice for science on societal issues;
- Promote the responsible use of science in public policy;
- Strengthen and diversify the science and technology workforce;
- Foster education in science and technology for everyone;
- Increase public engagement with science and technology; and
- Advance international cooperation in science.

For more information about the American Association for the Advancement of Science (AAAS), visit their website at www.aaas.org.

American Association for Cancer Research

The American Association for Cancer Research was founded in 1907 by a small group of physicians and scientists interested in research "to further the investigation and spread the knowledge of cancer." Today, the American Association for Cancer Research is known as the world's oldest and largest scientific organization focused on all aspects of high-quality, innovative cancer research.

The American Association for Cancer Research states on their website that their mission is: "to prevent and cure cancer through research, education, communication, and collaboration. Through its programs and services, the AACR fosters research in cancer and related biomedical science; accelerates the dissemination of new research findings among scientists and others dedicated to the conquest of cancer, promotes science education and training; and advances the understanding of the causes of cancer etiology, prevention, diagnosis, and treatment throughout the world."

For more information about the American Association for Cancer Research, visit their website at www.aacr.org.

American Association of Immunologists (AAI)

Known to be the largest and most prestigious professional association for immunologists worldwide, the American Association of Immunologists (AAI) is a professional association who states on their website that their purpose is "to advance the knowledge of immunology and related disciplines, to foster interchange of ideas and information among investigators in the various disciplines and to promote an understanding of the field of immunology." Some of the activities of AAI include: sharing information about advances in immunology (through their publication of *The Journal of Immunology*); holding an annual international meeting on immunology; offering professional development opportunities and hosting both introductory and advanced courses on immunology; recognizing scientists who have made significant contributions in the field through sponsored awards programs; offering fellowship programs for high school and college science teachers; and interacting with other organizations, government agencies, and legislators to promote the importance of biomedical research and the field of immunology.

For more information about the American Association of Immunologists (AAI), visit their website at www.aai.org.

American Association of Pharmaceutical Scientists (AAPS)

Founded in 1986, the American Association of Pharmaceutical Scientists (AAPS) is a professional, scientific association with members employed in industry, academia, government, and other research institutes worldwide. The Association states on its website that its mission is to provide "a dynamic international forum for the exchange of knowledge among scientists to enhance their contribution to health" and "to offer timely scientific programs, ongoing education, opportunities for networking, and professional development."

The Association also shares their vision to "be the premier organization of scientists devoted to the discovery, development, and manufacture of pharmaceutical products and therapies through the advances in science and technology."

For more information about the American Association of Pharmaceutical Scientists (AAPS), visit their website at www.aaps.org.

American Biological Safety Association (ABSA)

The American Biological Safety Association (ABSA) was founded in 1984 to promote biosafety as a scientific discipline and serve the increasing needs of biosafety professionals throughout the world. The goals of ABSA are to provide a professional association that represents the interests and needs of these specialists and provide an environment for the exchange and communication of information.

The American Biological Safety Association states on their website in their mission statement that they are "dedicated to expanding biological safety awareness to prevent adverse occupational and environmental impact from biohazards." They also share their goals to:

- Expand professional and public awareness of biological safety through effective communication.
- Participate in the development of biological safety and biosecurity standards, guidelines, and regulations.
- Develop themselves as the recognized resource for professional and scientific expertise in biological safety and biosecurity.
- Advance biological safety as a scientific discipline through education, research, and professional development.

For more information about the American Biological Safety Association (ABSA), visit their website at www.absa.org.

American Chemical Society (ACS)

Founded in 1876 and with members in all fields of chemistry, chemical engineering, and related sciences, the American Chemical Society (ACS), a non-profit organization holding a congressional charter, considers themselves to be the world's largest scientific society and one of the leading sources of authoritative scientific information.

The Society plays a significant role in educating and communicating with public policy makers and the general public about the importance of chemistry in our lives which includes identifying new solutions, improving public health, protecting the environment and contributing to the economy.

As stated on their website, the Society is committed to "improving people's lives through the transforming power of chemistry" and their mission is: "to advance the broader chemistry enterprise and its practitioners for the benefit of Earth and its people."

For more information about the American Chemical Society, visit their website at www.acs.org.

American Geological Institute (AGI)

Founded in 1948, the American Geosciences Institute (AGI) is a nonprofit federation of 50 geoscience societies and professional associations that serves the geoscience community geologists, geophysicists, and other earth and environmental scientists. The institute provides information and education services to its members and the community while promoting a united voice for the community and striving to increase public awareness of the vital role the geosciences play in society's use of resources, resilience to natural hazards, and the health of the environment.

For more about the American Geological Institute (AGI) visit their website at www.agiweb.org.

American Heart Association (AHA)

The American Heart Association (AHA) is a non-profit organization that promotes appropriate cardiac care in an effort to reduce disability and deaths related to cardiovascular disease and stroke. They are a national voluntary health agency who states on their website that their mission is: "... to build healthier lives, free of cardiovascular diseases and stroke. That single purpose drives all we do. The need for our work is beyond question."

The American Heart Association publishes a standard for providing basic and advanced life support, including standards for the proper performance of cardiopulmonary resuscitation (CPR); offers the most widely accepted certification for basic life support (BLS); and is now a provider of training for first aid.

The AHA also operates an affiliated organization, the American Stroke Association, which focuses on the care, research and prevention of strokes (www.strokeassociation.org).

For more about the American Heart Association (AHA), visit their website at www.heart.org.

American Institute of Biological Sciences

Founded in 1947 as a part of the National Academy of Sciences, the American Institute of Biological Sciences (AIBS) became an independent, member-governed organization in the 1950s. The American Institute of Biological Sciences is a nonprofit 501(c)(3) scientific association that works to ensure that the public, members of the legislature, funders, and the community of biologists have access to and use information that will guide them in making informed decisions and solving problems about related matters.

The American Institute of Biological Sciences (AIBS) states on their website that they are "dedicated to advancing biological research and education for the welfare of society. AIBS seeks to facilitate communication and interactions among biologists, professional biological societies, and biological and other scientific disciplines, as well as to serve and advance the interests of biology in the broader scientific community and in other components of society."

Some of the goals of the Association include: facilitating communication and interaction, serving as a national representative and forum for biology and biologists, and enhancing biological research, education, and communication.

172

For more information about the American Institute of Biological Sciences (AIBS), visit their website at www. aibs.org.

American Institute of Chemical Engineers

Founded in 1908 with the purpose of establishing chemical engineers as a profession independent from chemists and mechanical engineers, AIChE considers themselves to be the world's leading organization for chemical engineering professionals. AIChE has the extent of resources and expertise you need whether you are in core process industries or emerging areas, such as nanobiotechnology.

At the time AIChE was founded, chemical engineering was emerging from its roots in the chemistry industry. AIChE has helped to establish the discipline of chemical engineering and provides a foundation for a constantly evolving and vital profession.

Over the years members have worked on notable achievements, established accreditation standards for chemical engineering programs and continue setting guidelines for government agencies assisting AIChE in making significant, lasting contributions to society and the world.

As stated on their website, the mission of the Institute is to:

- Promote excellence in chemical engineering education and global practice
- Advance the development and exchange of relevant knowledge
- Uphold and advance the profession's standards, ethics and diversity
- Enhance the lifelong career development and financial security of chemical engineers through products, services, networking, and advocacy
- Stimulate collaborative efforts among industry, universities, government, and professional societies
- Encourage other engineering and scientific professionals to participate in AIChE activities
- Advocate public policy that embraces sound technical and economic information and that represents the interest of chemical engineers
- Facilitate public understanding of technical issues; and
- Achieve excellence in operations of the Institute.

For more information about the American Institute of Chemical Engineers (AIChE), visit their website at www.aiche.org.

American Society for Horticultural Science (ASHS)

Founded in 1903, the American Society for Horticultural Science (ASHS) is "the largest, most visible organization dedicated to advancing all facets of horticultural research, education, and application." The ASHS provides a foundation for research and education in horticulture and strives for the advancement of horticultural science. The Society "supports science for specialty crops: global solutions for nutritious food sources and healthy, beautiful environments." Its members continue to make significant advances in the areas of research and education.

For more information about the American Society for Horticultural Science (ASHS), visit their website at www.ashs.org.

American Society for Clinical Investigation

Established in 1098, The American Society for Clinical Investigation (ASCI) is one of the nation's oldest and most respected medical honor societies and is home to physician-scientists from all medical specialties who are elected to the Society for their outstanding records of scholarly achievement in biomedical research. Many of their senior members are widely recognized leaders in academic medicine.

The ASCI states on their website that they are "dedicated to the advancement of research that extends our understanding and improves the treatment of human diseases, and members are committed to mentoring future generations of physician-scientists." Each year the ASCI considers the nominations of several hundred physician-scientists from the United States and abroad and elects up to 80 new members for their significant research accomplishments. Members typically must be 45 years of age or younger at the time of their election so their membership reflects the accomplishments by its members fairly early in their careers.

For more information about the American Society for Clinical Investigation (ASCI), visit their website at www.the-asci.org.

American Society for Clinical Laboratory Science

Over many decades the American Society for Clinical Laboratory Science (ASCLS) has contributed a great deal to the profession and practitioners in clinical laboratory science. They have contributed in advocacy, standards setting, education (professional and continuing), and personal and professional development. The American Society for Clinical Laboratory Science (ASCLS) continues today as one of the highest ranking laboratory organizations representing laboratory personnel and advancing their interests — individually and collectively.

As stated on their website, the mission of the Society is: "to make a positive impact in health care through leadership that will assure excellence in the practice of laboratory medicine."

For more information about the American Society for Clinical Laboratory Science (ASCLS), visit their website at www.ascls.org.

American Society for Microbiology (ASM)

Founded in 1899 (originally under the name "Society of American Bacteriologists") the American Society for Microbiology (ASM) is a professional organization whose members represent 26 disciplines of microbiological specialization as well as microbiology educations.

As stated on their website, the mission of the Academy is: "to advance the microbiological sciences as a vehicle for understanding life processes and to apply and communicate this knowledge for the improvement of health and environmental and economic well being worldwide."

They also indicate that to achieve these goals, ASM will:

- Support programs of education, training and public information;
- Publish journals and books; convene meetings, workshops and colloquia;
- Promote the contributions and promise of the microbiological sciences;
- Recognize achievement and distinction among its practitioners;
- Set standards of ethical and professional behavior.

For more information about the American Society for Microbiology (ASM), visit their website at www.asm.org.

American Association of Petroleum Geologists (AAPG)

Founded in 1917, the American Association of Petroleum Geologists (AAPG) is one of the world's largest professional geological societies. Since its founding, the American Association of Petroleum Geologists has been a leader in the world-wide scientific community. The membership of AAPG includes geologists, geophysicists, CEOs, managers, consultants, students and academicians. The Association states on their website that their original mission, "to foster scientific research, to advance the science of geology, to promote technology, and to inspire high professional conduct," still guides them today.

There are three divisions of the AAPG that focus on professionalism, alternative energy sources and the environment – the Division of Environmental Geosciences, Division of Professional Affairs, and the Energy and Minerals Division.

For more information about the American Association of Petroleum Geologists (AAPG), visit their website at www.aapg.org.

American Society of Agronomy

Founded in 1907, The American Society of Agronomy (ASA) is a prominent international scientific and professional society of agronomists and scientists of related disciplines. It was founded with the objective of "the increase and dissemination of knowledge concerning soils, crops, and the conditions affecting them." The ASA and its members devote themselves to the ongoing development of agriculture, enabled by science, in harmony with environmental and human values. The Society and its members support the scientific, educational and professional research needed to enhance productivity, technology and communication while sustaining the integrity of ecological processes that encompass crop science, soil science, and environmental science. The research is communicated and transferred among agronomists, scientists and others in related disciplines on topics of local, regional, national, and international significance.

Since its inception, ASA has continued to evolve, modifying its educational offerings to support the changing needs of its members. Today, ASA is seen as a progressive scientific society meeting the needs of its members through publications, recognition and awards, placement service, certification programs, meetings, and student activities.

Because of their common interests, ASA, the Crop Science Society of America (CSSA), and the Soil Science

Society of America (SSSA) share a close working relationship. Each of the three Societies is autonomous, has its own bylaws, and is governed by its own Board of Directors. These Societies are non-profit, educational organizations.

For more information about the American Society of Agronomy (ASA), visit their website at www.agronomy.org.

American Society for Clinical Pathology (ASCP)

Founded in 1922, the American Society for Clinical Pathology (ASCP) considers themselves to be the world's largest professional membership organization for pathologists and laboratory professionals with thousands of members working as pathologists, resident and other physicians, pathologists' assistants, laboratory professionals, medical student and laboratory students. The Society's influence has guided the application and evolution of the pathology and laboratory medicine specialty since its inception and is committed to providing excellence in education, certification and advocacy on behalf of patients, pathologists and laboratory professionals. The Society states on their website that their mission is "to be a unifying force for the laboratory team well known for its high quality, innovative programs and respected for its credibility and integrity."

For more information about the American Society for Clinical Pathology (ASCP), visit their website at www.ascp.org.

American Society of Human Genetics (ASHG)

Founded in 1948, the American Society of Human Genetics (ASHG) is the primary professional membership organization for human genetics specialists worldwide. As a membership organization, the ASHG includes multidisciplinary professionals with a common interest in human genetic research and clinical practice. The Society members include researchers, academicians, clinicians, laboratory practice professionals, genetic counselors, nurses and others who have a special interest in the field of human genetics. The members of ASHG contribute to the advancement of science for the benefit of health with a commitment to becoming fluent in the language of the genome, understanding human variation, and promoting the public health.

On their website, the American Society of Human Genetics shares the following with regard to their mission. The Society serves research scientists, health professionals, and the public by providing forums to:

- Share research results at annual meetings and in through their principal publication: *The American Journal of Human Genetics*
- Advance genetic research by advocating for research support
- Enhance genetics education by preparing future professionals and informing the public
- Promote genetic services and support responsible social and scientific policies

For more information about the American Society of Human Genetics (ASHG), visit their website at www. ashg.org.

Association of Clinical Research Professionals (ACRP)

Founded in 1976, the Association of Clinical Research Professionals (ACRP) is the primary resource for clinical research professionals in the pharmaceutical, biotechnology and medical device industries, as wells as for those in hospital, academic medical centers and physician office settings. The ACRP's original focus in 1976 was to address the individual educational and networking needs of research nurses and those supporting the work of clinical studies. With the establishment of the society came the recognition of a new profession – that of the clinical researcher. The Association is dedicated to clinical research and development and states their mission on their website to "provide global leadership to promote integrity and excellence for the clinical research profession."

For more information about the Association of Clinical Research Professionals (ACRP), visit their website at www.acrpnet.org.

Association for Project Management (APM)

Founded in 1972, the Association for Project Management (APM) is a registered charity in the United Kingdom who states on their website in their mission statement that their commitment is to "develop and promote the professional disciplines of project and programme management for the public benefit." The APM is committed to the highest standards of professional conduct and ethics for all project and program management professionals and within all segments of the industry. With over 19,000 individuals and 500 corporate members, APM is one of the largest professional associations of its kind throughout Europe.

For more information about the Association for Project Management (APM) visit their website at www.apm.org.

Association of Women in Science

The Association for Women in Science was founded in 1971 when the American Societies for Experimental Biology (FASEB) invited women scientists to a meeting to encourage the exchange of ideas and solutions to overcoming job discrimination, lower pay, and professional isolation. As one of the largest multidisciplinary science organizations for women, the Association for Women in Sciences (AWIS) is a leadership organization supporting the interests of women in science and technology.

On their website the AWIS shares this mission statement: "AWIS champions the interests of women in science, technology engineering and mathematics across all disciplines and employment sectors. Working for positive system transformation, AWIS strives to ensure that all women in these fields can achieve their full potential."

In an effort to promote the entrance and advancement of women in science, AWIS is committed to nurturing the careers of women science professionals. With 49 chapters of members nationwide, AWIS serves as local networks and mentoring groups for professionals in every stage of their careers, bringing together scientists with students and young women and girls who are considering careers in these fields. They work at the national level as wells as through its chapters to promote equity, workplace best practices and diversity.

For more information about the Association of Women in Science (AWIS), visit their website at www.awis.org.

Biomedical Engineering Society (BMES)

The Biomedical Engineering Society (BMES), a 501(c)3 nonprofit professional association, was incorporated in 1968 in response to the need to provide a society offering equal status to representatives of both biomedical and engineering interests and was established to serve as the lead society and professional home for biomedical engineering and bioengineering students, academics, and professionals. With a membership of approximately 4,000 and with almost 100 student chapters and several emerging industry and international chapters, BMES seeks to serve as the world's leading society of professionals dedicated to the promotion and enhancement of biomedical engineering knowledge worldwide and its utilization for human health and well-being.

The Biomedical Engineering Society states on their website that their mission is "to build and support the biomedical engineering community, locally, nationally, and internationally, with activities designed to communicate recent advances, discoveries, and inventions; promote education and professional development; and integrate the perspectives of the academic, medical, governmental, and business sectors."

For more information about the Biomedical Engineering Society (BMES), visit their website at www.bmes.org.

Biophysical Society

Founded in 1957 and with members who work in the areas of academia, industry and in worldwide government agencies, the Biophysical Society encourages the development and dissemination of knowledge in biophysics through its many activities including meetings, publications (twice monthly *Biophysical Journal*, monthly *Biophysical Society Newsletter* as well as various Annual Meeting Publications), community outreach, career placement and committee outreach programs. Membership is open to scientists who share the vision of the

Society and who have educational, research, or practical experience in biophysics or related scientific field.

For more information about the Biophysical Society, visit their website at www.biophysics.org.

Biotechnology Industry Organization (BIO)

Created in 1993 through the merger of the Association of Biotechnology Companies and the Industrial Biotechnology Association, the Biotechnology Industry Organization's goal was for the entire biotechnology industry, from startups to established companies, to speak with one voice for the industry on important policy issues. As the world's largest biotechnology organization, the Biotechnology Industry Organization (BIO) provides advocacy, business development and communications services for more than 1,100 members worldwide. Their members are involved in the research and development of innovative healthcare, agricultural, industrial and environmental biotechnology products. As the BIO states on their website, their mission is: to be "the champion of biotechnology and the advocate for its member organizations – both large and small."

BIO represents state and regional biotech associations, service providers to the industry, and academic centers and includes corporate members ranging from entrepreneurial companies to Fortune 500 corporations.

For more information about the Biotechnology Industry Organization (BIO), visit their website at www.bio.org.

Botanical Society of America (BSA)

Established in 1893, the Botanical Society of America (BSA) was a branch of the Botanical Club of the American Association of the Advancement of Science. In 1906 it became a larger association of plant scientists with the merging of the Society for Plant Morphology and Physiology and the American Mycological Society. Its members include scientists, professors, teachers, students, botanists and individuals interested in the fields of botany and/or plants.

As stated on their website, the society's mission is to: "promote botany, the field of basic science dealing with the study and inquiry into the form, function, development, diversity, reproduction, evolution, and uses of plants and their interactions within the biosphere."

For more information about the Botanical Society of America (BSA), visit their website at www.botany.org.

Center for Biotechnology at Stonybrook

Established in 1983, the Center for Biotechnology at Stonybrook (CFB) is designated as a New York State Center for Advanced Technology (CAT) in Medical Biotechnology. The Center was established as a cooperative research and development partnership between universities, private industry and government. The Center's primary objective is to generate positive economic impact in the form of new and retained jobs, corporate revenues and cost savings, as well as leveraged funding from private and public sources, primarily by capitalizing on the unique research capabilities of academic institutions to drive and support a globally competitive, knowledge-based economy in New York State.

To accomplish their goal, the Center has developed a comprehensive and multi-faceted strategy, the implementation of which includes a wide scope of programs and activities in infrastructure development, technology development, business development, and workforce development.

The Center seeks to support collaborative research arrangements between industry and academia. They have extensive collaborative agreements with New York's biotechnology industry, as well as national and international biotechnology and pharmaceutical firms.

As stated on their website, the mission of the Center for Biotechnology (CFB) is to: "catalyze the translation of basic biomedical sciences into diagnostic and therapeutic technologies that benefit human health and society, and fuel economic growth."

For more information about the Center for Biotechnology at Stonybrook, visit their website at www.biotech. sunysb.edu.

Crop Science Society of America

The Crop Science Society of America (CSSA) is a non-profit educational and scientific organization dedicated to the advancement of crop science. Because of their common interests, CSSA, the American Society of Agronomy (ASA), and the Soil Science Society of America (SSSA) share a close working relationship, each maintaining its own bylaws and governed by its own Board of Directors. Members of these Societies are dedicated to the conservation and sensible use of natural resources to produce food, feed, fuel, fiber crops, and pharmaceutical crops while maintaining and improving the environment and are dedicated to the acquisition and dissemination of knowledge that advances the sciences and professions.

For more information about the Crop Science Society of America (CSSA), visit their website at www.crops.org.

Ecological Society of America (ESA)

Founded in 1915, the Ecological Society of America (ESA) is a nonprofit professional organization of ecological scientists. The Society seeks to promote ecological science by improving communication among ecologists, raising the public's awareness of the importance of ecological science, increasing the resources available for the conduct of ecological science, and ensuring the appropriate use of ecological science in environmental

189

decision making. The Ecological Society of America has over 10,000 members worldwide who are researchers, educators, natural resource managers, and students who use ecological science to address environmental issues. Some of the areas addressed by the Society members include biotechnology, natural resource management, ecological restoration, ozone depletion and global climate change, ecosystem management, species extinction and loss of biological diversity, habitat alteration and destruction, and sustainable ecological systems.

For more information about the Ecological Society of America (ESA), visit their website at www.esa.org.

European Medicines Agency (EMA)

Set up in 1995 with funding from the European Union and pharmaceutical industry and member states, the European Medicines Agency (EMA) is a decentralized scientific agency responsible for the scientific evaluation of medicines developed by pharmaceutical companies for use in the European Union and is responsible for coordinating the existing scientific resources put at its disposal by Member States for the evaluation, supervision and pharmacovigilance of medicinal products. The Agency states that its main responsibility is "the protection and promotion of public and animal health, through the evaluation and supervision of medicines for human and veterinary use."

The Agency provides the Member States and the institutions of the European Union the best-possible scientific advice relating to the evaluation of the quality, safety and efficacy of medicinal products for human or veterinary use referred to it in accordance with the provisions of EU legislation relating to medicinal products.

Working with the Member States and the European Commission as partners in a European medicines network, the Agency:

- provides independent, science-based recommendations on the quality, safety and efficacy of medicines, and on issues relevant to public and animal health that involve medicines;
- applies efficient and transparent evaluation procedures to help bring new medicines to the market by means of a single, European marketing authorisation;
- implements measures for continuously supervising the quality, safety and efficacy of authorised medicines to ensure that their benefits outweigh their risks;
- provides scientific advice and incentives to stimulate the development and improve the availability of innovative new medicines;
- recommends safe limits for residues of veterinary medicines used in food-producing animals, for the establishment of maximum residue limits by the European Commission;
- involves representatives of patients, healthcare professionals and other stakeholders in its work, to facilitate dialogue on issues of common interest;
- publishes impartial and comprehensible information about medicines and their use;
- develops best practice for medicines evaluation and supervision in Europe, and contributes

alongside the Member States and the European Commission to the harmonisation of regulatory standards at the international level.

The European Medicines Agency is similar to the US Food and Drug Administration (FDA), but without FDA-type centralization.

As stated on their website, the mission of the European Medicines Agency is "to foster scientific excellence in the evaluation and supervision of medicines, for the benefit of public and animal health."

For more information about the European Medicines Agency (EMA), visit their website at www.emea.europa.eu.

Federation of American Scientists (FAS)

Founded in 1945, the Federation of American Scientists (FAS) is a nonpartisan, 501(c)(3) non-profit organization. The Federation states on its website that its members are "dedicated to providing rigorous, objective, evidence-based analysis and practical policy recommendations on national and international security issues connected to applied science and technology." In addition, they state that they are "committed to educating policymakers, the public, the news media, and the next generation of scientists, engineers, and global leaders about the urgent need for creating a more secure and better world."

The Federation was founded by scientists who worked on the Manhattan Project to develop the first atomic bombs. These scientists recognized that science had become central to many key public policy questions. They also believed that scientists had a unique responsibility to both warn the public and policy leaders of potential dangers from scientific and technical advances and to show how good policy could increase the benefits of new scientific knowledge.

Initially devoted to the prevention of nuclear war and with nuclear security as a main objective, the organization has expanded its work to include the issues of biosecurity, building technologies, conventional arms sales monitoring, energy security, government secrecy, international science partnerships, learning technologies, and terrorism analysis.

For more information about the Federation of American Scientists (FAS), visit their website at www.fas.org.

Federation of American Societies for Experimental Biology (FASEB)

Founded in 1912, the Federation of American Societies for Experimental Biology (FASEB) was established to provide a forum in which to hold educational meetings, develop publications, and disseminate biological research results. Originally created by as a small group of dedicated scientists, the federation has grown to be the nation's largest coalition of biomedical researchers;

it represents 26 scientific societies and over 100,000 researchers from around the world.

As stated on their website, the mission of the Federation of American Societies for Experimental Biology (FASEB) is to: "advance health and welfare by promoting progress and education in biological and biomedical sciences through service to our member societies and collaborative advocacy."

For more information about the Federation of American Societies for Experimental Biology (FASEB), visit their website at www.faseb.org.

Food and Drug Administration (FDA)

The Food and Drug Administration (FDA) is an agency within US Department of Health and Human Services and is responsible for: protecting and promoting public health by assuring the safety, efficacy, and security of human and veterinary drugs, biological products, medical devices, the nation's food supply, cosmetics, and products that emit radiation; for advancing the public health by helping to speed innovations that make medicines more effective, safer, and more affordable and by helping the public get the accurate, science-based information they need to use medicines and foods to maintain and improve their health; and for regulating the manufacturing, marketing and distribution of tobacco products to protect the public health and to reduce tobacco use by minors.

The FDA's organization provides the public with information to promote the safe and appropriate within the following divisions:

The Center for Biologics Evaluation and Research

The Center for Biologics Evaluation and Research (CBER) is the Center within the FDA that regulates biological products for human use under applicable federal laws. CBER protects and advances the public health by ensuring that biological products are safe and effective and available to those who need them and also provides the public with information to promote the safe and appropriate use of biological products.

The Center for Devices and Radiological Health

The FDA's Center for Devices and Radiological Health (CDRH) is responsible for regulating firms who manufacture, repackage, re-label, and/or import medical devices sold in the United States. CDRH also regulates radiation-emitting electronic products (medical and non-medical) such as lasers, x-ray systems, ultrasound equipment, microwave ovens and color televisions.

The Center for Drug Evaluation and Research

The Center for Drug Evaluation and Research (CDER) performs an essential public health task by making sure that safe and effective drugs are available to improve the health of people in the United States. CDER regulates over-the-counter and prescription drugs, including biological therapeutics and generic drugs. This work covers more than just medicines. For example, fluoride toothpaste, antiperspirants, dandruff shampoos and sunscreens are all considered "drugs."

The Center for Food Safety and Applied Nutrition

The Center for Food Safety and Applied Nutrition (CFSAN) is one of six product-oriented centers at the FDA and is a scientific regulatory agency responsible for the safety of the nation's domestically produced and imported foods, cosmetics, drugs, biologics, medical devices, and radiological products.

The Center provides services to consumers, domestic and foreign industry and other outside groups regarding field programs; agency administrative tasks; scientific analysis and support; and policy, planning and handling of critical issues related to food and cosmetics.

The Center for Tobacco Products

The Center for Tobacco Products (CTP) oversees the implementation of the Family Smoking Prevention and Tobacco Control Act. Some of the Agency's responsibilities under the law include setting performance standards, reviewing premarket applications for new and modified risk tobacco products, requiring new warning labels, and establishing and enforcing advertising and promotion restrictions.

The Center for Veterinary Medicine

The Center for Veterinary Medicine (CVM) regulates the manufacture and distribution of food additives and drugs that will be given to animals. CVM is responsible for regulating drugs, devices, and food additives given to, or used on, over one hundred million companion animals, plus millions of poultry, cattle, swine, and minor animal species (animals other than cattle, swine, chickens, turkeys, horses, dogs, and cats).

The National Center for Toxicological Research

The National Center for Toxicological Research (NCTR), FDA's internationally recognized research center, plays a critical role in the FDA's mission. The unique scientific expertise of NCTR is critical in supporting FDA product centers and their regulatory roles.

The National Center for Toxicological Research (NCTR) is an important research component of the FDA that plays a critical role in the missions of FDA and DHHS to promote and protect public health.

- NCTR – in partnership with researchers from government, academia, and industry – develops, refines, and applies current and emerging technologies to improve safety evaluations of FDA-regulated products.
- NCTR fosters national and international collaborations to improve and protect public health and enhance the quality of life for the American people. Through the training of scientists from

around the world, as well as FDA staff, NCTR researchers spread the principles of regulatory science globally.

- NCTR conducts FDA research with the goal to develop a scientifically sound basis for regulatory decisions and reduce risks associated with FDA-regulated products. NCTR represents the FDA on key committees of the National Toxicology Program (NTP), a program that evaluates the effects of chemicals on health. Over the past 30 years, the NTP and NCTR have conducted studies on FDA-nominated compounds, providing data to support science-based regulatory decisions.

The Office of Regulatory Affairs

The FDA's Office of Regulatory Affairs is the lead office for all FDA Field activities as well as providing FDA leadership on imports, inspections, and enforcement policy. ORA supports the five FDA Product Centers by inspecting regulated products and manufacturers, conducting sample analysis on regulated products, and reviewing imported products offered for entry into the United States. ORA also develops FDA-wide policy on compliance and enforcement and executes FDA's Import Strategy and Food Protection Plans.

Besides executing its mission through its Federal workforce, ORA also works with its State, Local, Tribal, and Territories counterparts to further FDA's mission. ORA funds grants and cooperative agreements to perform State inspections and provide technical assistance to the States in such areas as milk, food, and shellfish safety.

For more information about the Food and Drug Administration (FDA), visit their website at www.fda.org.

Genetics Society of America (GSA)

Established in 1931, the Genetics Society of America (GSA) is a scholarly membership society of genetics researchers and educators who endeavor to be the collective voice of its members and who seeks to foster a unified science of genetics and to maximize its intellectual and practical impact. The GSA states on their website that the purposes of the Society are: "1) to facilitate communication between geneticists, 2) to promote research that will bring new discoveries in genetics, 3) to foster the training of the next generation of geneticists so they can effectively respond to the opportunities provided by our discoveries and the challenges posed by them, and 4) to educate the public and their government representatives about advances in genetics and the consequences to individuals and to society."

For more information about the Genetics Society of America (GSA), visit their website at www.genetics-gsa.org.

Infectious Disease Society of America (IDSA)

Formed in 1963, the Infectious Diseases Society of America (IDSA) represents physicians, scientists and health care professionals who specialize in infectious diseases. The over 9,000 members of the Society include practicing clinicians, scientists and researchers in the academic setting, public health officials, hospital epidemiologists, and Infectious Disease specialists. The Society states on its website that its purpose is to: "improve the health of individuals, communities, and society by promoting excellence in patient care, education, research, public health, and prevention relating to infectious diseases."

For more information about the Infectious Disease Society of America (IDSA),visit their website at www.idsociety.org.

Institute of Food Technologists (IFT)

The Institute of Food Technologies (IFT) was founded in 1939 and includes members from nearly every discipline related to food science and technology. The scientists believe that the communication among professionals involved in food science and technology is essential to the progress of these disciplines.

The Institute states on their website that they exist "to advance the science of food" and that their "long-range vision is to ensure a safe and abundant food supply contributing to healthier people everywhere."

For more information about the Institute of Food Technologists (IFT), visit their website at www.ift.org.

International Organization for Standardization (ISO)

Founded in 1947, the International Organization for Standardization (ISO) was originally known as the International Federation of the National Standardizing Association (ISA) with its focus being "to facilitate the international coordination and unification of industrial standards." The ISA was disbanded in 1942 but was reorganized in 1946 under its current name. The ISO is an international standard-setting organization that includes representatives from various national standards organizations and disseminates worldwide proprietary, industrial and commercial standards. With its 162 national members, the ISO states on its website that its objectives include:

- making the development, manufacturing and supply of products and services more efficient, safer and cleaner,
- facilitating the trade between countries and making it fairer,
- providing governments with a technical base for health, safety and environmental legislation, and conformity assessment,
- sharing technological advances and good management practice,
- disseminating innovation,
- safeguarding consumers, and users in general, of products and services, and
- making life simpler by providing solutions to common problems.

For more information about the International Organization for Standardization (ISO), visit their website at www.iso.org.

International Society for Pharmaceutical Engineers (ISPE)

Founded in 1980 by a group of individuals who believed the pharmaceutical industry needed an organization that would deal with practical applications of science and technology for technical professionals, the International Society for Pharmaceutical Engineers (ISPE) focused on improving efficiency and best practices. With 22,000 members in 90 countries worldwide, the Society continues to work to keep industry professionals informed of the latest technological and regulatory trends and is committed to the advancement the education and technical efficiency of its members. The ISPE seeks to promote advancement in the pharmaceutical industry by providing professionals with opportunities in the development of technical knowledge, exchanging of practical experience, and collaborating with global regulatory agencies and industry leaders.

For more information about the International Society for Pharmaceutical Engineers (ISPE), visit their website at www.ispe.org.

Licensing Executives Society (LES)

Established in 1965, the Licensing Executives Society (U.S.A. and Canada), Inc. (LES) is a professional society with members who engage in the transfer, use, development and marketing of intellectual property.

The LES membership includes a wide range of professionals, including business executives, lawyers, licensing consultants, engineers, academicians, scientists and government officials. Many large corporations, professional firms, and universities comprise the Society's membership.

The Society states on its website that its mission is:

- To encourage high standards and ethics among persons engaged in licensing, other transfers of technology, and intellectual property rights.
- To assist members in improving their skills and techniques in licensing, other transfers of technology, and intellectual property rights through education, publications and exchange of ideas.
- To inform the business community and governmental bodies of the economic significance and importance of licensing, other transfers of technology, and intellectual property rights and the high professional standards of those engaged in the profession.
- To assist in furthering the employment of technology through licensing and other transfers of intellectual property.

The Licensing Executives Society (U.S.A. and Canada), Inc. (LES) is a member society of the Licensing Executives Society International, Inc. (LESI), with a worldwide membership of over 12,000 members in 30 national societies, representing over 80 countries.

For more information about the Licensing Executives Society (LES), visit their website at www.lesusacanada. org.

Licensing Executives Society International (LESI)

The Licensing Executives Society International (LESI) is an association of 32 national and regional societies, composed of individuals who have an interest in the transfer of technology, or licensing of intellectual property rights – from technical know how and patented inventions to software, copyright and trademarks.

The LES family is, for the most part, business-oriented and has 10,000 individual members that include management representatives from companies both large, medium and small, scientists, engineers, academicians, governmental officials, lawyers, patent and trademark attorneys and consultants.

On 30 June 2000 LES International was incorporated and its official name since then is LES International, Inc.

As indicated on its website, LES International states it objectives as:

1. To function as a non-profit professional society encouraging high professional standards among individuals engaged in the transfer and licensing of technology and industrial or intellectual property rights.
2. To assist its members in improving their skills and techniques in licensing through self education, the conduct of special studies and research, the sponsorship of educational meetings, the publication of statistics, reports, articles and other material, and the exchange of ideas related to domestic and foreign licensing.
3. To inform the public, international bodies, governmental bodies, and the business community concerning the economic significance of licensing and the high professional standards of those engaged in the licensing profession.
4. To make available to its members the latest, most accurate, information on licensing.

For more information about the Licensing Executives Society International (LESI), visit their website at www.lesi.org.

Marine Technology Society (MTS)

Incorporated in 1963, the Marine Technology Society (MTS) was established to give members of academia, government and industry a common forum for the exchange of information and ideas in the marine sciences.

Their purpose is: "To promote awareness, understanding, advancement and application of marine technology." Their members include businesses, institutions, individual professionals and students who are ocean engineers, technologists, policy makers and educators.

As stated on their website, the mission of the Society is to:

- Facilitate a broader understanding of the relevance of marine technology to wider global issues by enhancing the dissemination of marine technology information
- Promote and improve marine technology and related educational programs
- Advance the development of the tools and procedures required to explore, study and further the responsible and sustainable use of the oceans.

For more information about the Marine Technology Society (MTS), visit their website at www.mtsociety.org.

Materials Research Society (MRS)

Founded in 1973, the Materials Research Society (MRS) is a non-profit organization, consisting of over 16,000 members of scientists, engineers and research managers from industry, government, academia and research laboratories, that encourages communication and technical information exchange across the various fields of science affecting materials. The organization states on its website that it seeks to "promote communication for the advancement of interdisciplinary materials research to improve the quality of life."

For more information about the Materials Research Society (MRS), visit their website at www.mrs.org.

Microscopy Society of America

Founded in 1942, the Microscopy Society of America is a non-profit organization dedicated to the promotion and advancement of techniques and applications of microscopy and microanalysis in all relevant scientific disciplines.

The Microscopy Society of America will provide leadership for the discovery and dissemination of information about microscopy and microanalysis, especially in relation to the following multidisciplinary areas:

- Latest Developments in Instrumentation
- Emerging Trends in Characterization
- Discovering the Big World of Micro through Education and Outreach
- Uncovering the Inner Secrets of Life and Biological Sciences
- Exploring the Physical and Materials Sciences
- Resources for NanoScience and NanoTechnology

For more information about the Microscopy Society of America, visit their website at www.microscopy.org.

National Academy of Sciences (NAS)

Founded in 1863, the National Academy of Sciences (NAS) is a private, non-profit membership organization that elects the nation's leading scientists, engineers, and medical professionals and is "dedicated to furtherance of science and technology and to their use for the public good." The Society consists of members and foreign associates each of who are a part of 31 disciplinary Sections that include physical and mathematical sciences, biological sciences, engineering and applied sciences, biomedical sciences, behavioral and social sciences, and applied biological, agricultural and environmental sciences. As science began to play an ever-increasing role in national priorities and public life, the National Academy of Sciences expanded to include the National Research Council in 1916, the National Academy of Engineering in 1964, and the Institute of Medicine in 1970.

Members are elected to the National Academy of Sciences in recognition of their distinguished and continuing achievements in original research. Membership is a widely accepted mark of excellence in science and is considered one of the highest honors that a scientist can receive.

For more information about the National Academy of Sciences (NAS), visit their website at www.nasonline.org.

National Association of Environmental Professionals (NAEP)

The National Association of Environmental Professionals (NAEP) is a multi-disciplinary association for professionals dedicated to the advancement of the environmental professions and, as stated on their website, their mission is "to be the interdisciplinary organization dedicated to developing the highest standards of ethics and proficiency in the environmental professions." They are a forum for state-of-the-art information on environmental planning, research and management; a network of professional contacts and exchange of information among colleagues in industry, government, academia, as well as the private sector; a resource for structured career development from student memberships to certification as an environmental professional; and a proponent of ethics and the highest standards of practice in the environmental professions.

For more information about the National Association of Environmental Professionals (NAEP), visit their website at www.naep.org.

National Science Foundation (NSF)

Created by Congress in 1950, the National Science Foundation (NSF) is an independent federal agency who indicates on their website that their mission is "to promote the progress of science; to advance the national health, prosperity, and welfare; to secure the national defense" through research programs and education projects and by providing "support for all fields of fundamental science and engineering, except for medical sciences." Their scope has expanded over the years to include the areas of social and behavioral sciences, engineering, and science and mathematics education. Today, the NSF is the only U.S. federal agency supporting *all* the non-medical fields of research.

For more information about the National Science Foundation (NSF), visit their website at www.nsf.gov.

National Society of Black Engineers (NSBE)

Founded in 1975, the National Society of Black Engineers (NSBE) is a 501(c)(3) non-profit association that is owned and managed by its members and is considered one of the largest student-governed organizations in the country. As stated on their website, the NSBE's mission is "to increase the number of culturally responsible black engineers who excel academically, succeed professionally and positively impact the community" and is dedicated to the academic and professional success of African-American engineering students and professionals offering its members academic excellence programs, scholarships, leadership training, professional development and access to career opportunities.

The Society also states that they strive to accomplish the following objectives for their organization:

- Stimulate and develop student interest in the various engineering disciplines
- Strive to increase the number of minority students studying engineering at both the undergraduate and graduate levels
- Encourage members to seek advanced degrees in engineering or related fields and to obtain professional engineering registrations
- Promote public awareness of engineering and the opportunities for Blacks and other minorities in that profession
- Function as a representative body on issues and developments that affect the careers of Black Engineers.

For more information about the National Society of Black Engineers (NSBE), visit their website at www.nsbe.org.

New York Biotechnology Association (NYBA)

The New York Biotechnology Association (NYBA) is a not-for-profit trade association dedicated to the development and growth of New York State based biotechnology related industries and institutions and to strengthening the competitiveness of New York State as a premier global location for biotechnology/biomedical research, education and industry.

As stated on their website, the Association's mission statement indicates that "the New York Biotechnology Associations supports the development and growth of

New York Sate's biotechnology industry, and serves its members and the biotechnology community by providing a network for information exchange, shared services, and collective action."

For more information about the New York Biotechnology Association (NYBA), visit their website at www. nyba.org.

Pharmaceutical Research and Manufacturers of America (PhRMA)

Founded in 1958, the Pharmaceutical Research and Manufacturers of America (PhRMA) (originally named the Pharmaceutical Manufacturers Association) represents the country's leading pharmaceutical research and biotechnology companies and is devoted to inventing medicines that allow patients to live longer, healthier, and more productive lives. As stated on their website, the mission of PhRMA's is "to conduct effective advocacy for public policies that encourage discovery of important new medicines for patients by pharmaceutical and biotechnology research companies." To accomplish this mission, PhRMA is dedicated to achieving these goals in Washington, the states and the world: "broad patient access to safe and effective medicines through a free market, without price controls; strong intellectual property incentives; and transparent, efficient regulation and a free flow of information to patients."

For more information about the Pharmaceutical Research and Manufacturers of America (PhRMA), visit their website at www.phrma.org.

Pharmaceutical Training International (PTI)

PTI is a global training company with over 60 interactive courses focusing on Regulatory Affairs, R&D, Clinical Development, Animal Health, Biopharmaceuticals, Fine Chemicals, Medical Devices, Generics, Agrochemicals and Manufacturing best practices.

For more information about Pharmaceutical Training International (PTI), visit their website at www.informaglobalevents.com/division/pti.

Radiation Research Society

The Radiation Research Society states on their website that their mission is "to promote original research in natural sciences relating to radiation, to facilitate the integration of different disciplines in the study of radiation effects, and to promote the diffusion of knowledge in these fields."

The Society also indicates that they seek to encourage the advancement of radiation research in all areas of the natural sciences, to facilitate cooperative research between the disciplines of physics, chemistry, biology and medicine in the study of the properties and effects of radiation, and to promote the dissemination of knowledge in these and related fields.

For more information about the Radiation Research Society, visit their website at www.radres.org.

Society for Neuroscience (SfN)

Founded in 1969, the Society for Neuroscience (SfN) is a nonprofit membership organization of scientists and physicians whose research is focused on the study of the brain and nervous system. Since its inception, the Society has grown and is considered to be the world's largest organization of scientists and physicians devoted to advancing understanding of the brain and nervous system.

The Society for Neuroscience's states on their website that their mission is to:

1. Advance the understanding of the brain and the nervous system by bringing together scientists of diverse backgrounds, by facilitating the integration of research directed at all levels of biological organization, and by encouraging translational research and the application of new scientific knowledge to develop improved disease treatments and cures.
2. Provide professional development activities, information, and educational resources for neuroscientists at all stages of their careers, including undergraduates, graduates, and postdoctoral

fellows, and increase participation of scientists from a diversity of cultural and ethnic backgrounds.

3. Promote public information and general education about the nature of scientific discovery and the results and implications of the latest neuroscience research. Support active and continuing discussions on ethical issues relating to the conduct and outcomes of neuroscience research.

4. Inform legislators and other policymakers about new scientific knowledge and recent developments in neuroscience research and their implications for public policy, societal benefit, and continued scientific progress.

For more information about the Society for Neuroscience (SfN), visit their website at www.sfn.org.

Society of Clinical Research Associates

The Society of Clinical Research Associates, Inc. is a nonprofit, professional organization dedicated to the continuing education and development of clinical research professionals. The Society states on their website that their mission is "to provide training, continuing education, and an internationally recognized certification program that promote quality clinical research to protect the welfare of research participants and improve global health."

For more information about the Society of Clinical Research Associates, visit their website at www.socra.org.

Society of Women Engineers (SWE)

Founded in 1950, the Society of Women Engineers (SWE) is a not-for-profit educational and service organization that enables women to succeed and advance in the field of engineering, and to be recognized for their contributions as engineers and leaders. SWE is the driving force that establishes engineering as a highly desirable career goal for women through a range of training and development programs, networking opportunities, scholarships, and outreach and advocacy activities.

The Society of Women Engineers' states on their website that their mission, originally adopted in 1986, is to "stimulate women to achieve full potential in careers as engineers and leaders, expand the image of the engineering profession as a positive force in improving the quality of life, and demonstrate the value of diversity."

The Society states that they are committed to:
- Developing women in engineering across socio-economic strata and occupational focus.
- Encouraging the interest and active participation of women and girls of under-represented ethnic groups, including African-Americans, Asian-Americans, Hispanics, Pacific Islanders, and Native Americans.
- Providing support to women which acknowledges and respects differences in family status, sexual orientation, age, and physical abilities.

For more information about the Society of Women Engineers (SWE), visit their website at www.swe.org.

Soil Science Society of America (SSSA)

Founded in 1936, the Soil Science Society of America (SSSA) is a progressive international scientific society that fosters the transfer of knowledge and practices to sustain global soils. The society is dedicated to advancing the field of soil science. It supports its members in providing research and information about soils in relation to crop production, environmental quality, ecosystem sustainability, bioremediation, waste management, recycling, and wise land use.

As stated on their website, the mission of the Society is: "1) to enhance the sustainability of soils, the environment, and society by integrating diverse scientific disciplines and principles in soil science for the wise stewardship of soil and natural resources, and 2) to advance the discovery, practice, and profession of soil science through excellence in the acquisition and application of knowledge to address challenges facing society, in the training and professional development of soil scientists, and in the education of, and communication to a diverse citizenry."

Because of their common interests, the Soil Science Society of America (SSSA), the American Society of Agronomy (ASA), and Crop Science Society of America (CSSA) share a close working relationship.

For more information about the Soil Science Society of America (SSSA), visit their website at www.soils.org.

Women Entrepreneurs in Science & Technology

Launched in 2000, the Women Entrepreneurs in Science & Technology (WEST) organization promotes the advancement of women in the business of science and technology and provides a forum for women in these industries to network and share information about career advancement and personal and professional development.

As stated on their website, WEST's mission "is a community that provides:

- forums that support our members to develop skills that advance them in achieving their full potential
- opportunities to initiate and cultivate professional and strategic relationships
- encouragement, inspiration and recognition of women's achievements in science, technology and entrepreneurial enterprises
- an environment that fosters the entrepreneurial spirit by encouraging innovative thinking, risk taking and professional agility."

For more information about Women Entrepreneurs in Science & Technology (WEST), visit their website at www.westorg.org.

14

Journals,
Publications and
Additional Resources

O ur previous chapter provided information with
regard to associations and professional groups.
In this chapter we would like to share with you
some of the journals and publications available from
them. We have also provided additional resources which
may be of interest to you. These brief descriptions have
been obtained from the websites which we have listed.

American Academy of Forensic Sciences

Journal of Forensic Sciences
www.aafs.org/journal-forensic-sciences

This peer-reviewed journal provides the latest information on the many disciplines represented in forensic sciences. The journal's comprehensive coverage includes: pathology and biology, toxicology, psychiatry and behavioral sciences, odontology, physical anthropology, jurisprudence, criminalistics, questioned documents, engineering sciences, and digital and multimedia sciences.

American Association for the Advancement of Science

The AAAS currently publishes three respected peer-reviewed journals:

Science
www.sciencemag.org

An international weekly science journal and a leading journal of original scientific research, global news, and commentary.

Science Signaling
stke.sciencemag.org

A peer-reviewed scientific journal that is published weekly, as well as an online resource and information management tool that enables experts and novices in cell signaling to find, organize, and utilize information relevant to processes of cellular regulation.

Science Translational Medicine
stm.sciencemag.org

An interdisciplinary medical journal established in October 2009. AAAS states that its focus is original, peer-reviewed, science-based research that successfully advances clinical medicine toward the goal of improving patients' lives.

In addition to peer-reviewed journals, AAAS has a collection of print and online resources for educators, students, early-career scientists and engineers, reporters, and the public.

American Association for Cancer Research

Visit the many publications of AACR at: www.aacr.org/home/scientists/publications-of-the-aacr.aspx.

Their journals include:

Cancer Discovery
Cancer Research
Clinical Cancer Research
Cancer Epidemiology, Biomarkers & Prevention
Molecular Cancer Therapeutics
Molecular Cancer Research
Cancer Prevention Research

Cancer Reviews Online (CRO)
Cancer Prevention Journals Portal (CPJP)

AACR also provides their "OnlineFirst: Ahead of Print" publications which are listed below. OnlineFirst articles are published online before they appear in a regular issue of the journal.

Cancer Discovery OnLineFirst
http://cancerdiscovery.aacrjournals.org/content/early/by/section

Cancer Research OnLineFirst
http://cancerres.aacrjournals.org/content/early/recent

Clinical Cancer Research OnLineFirst
http://clincancerres.aacrjournals.org/content/early/recent

Cancer Epidemiology, Biomarkers & Prevention OnLineFirst
http://cebp.aacrjournals.org/content/early/recent

Molecular Cancer Therapeutics OnLineFirst
http://mct.aacrjournals.org/content/early/recent

Molecular Cancer Research OnLineFirst-
http://mcr.aacrjournals.org/content/early/recent

Cancer Prevention Research OnLineFirst
http://cancerpreventionresearch.aacrjournals.org/content/early/recent

American Association of Immunologists

The Journal of Immunology
www.jimmunol.org/

This journal provides peer-reviewed findings in all areas of experimental immunology including both basic and clinical studies.

American Association of Petroleum Geologists

AAPG Explorer
www.aapg.org/explorer/

This monthly newspaper includes coverage in all areas of energy interest, with emphasis on exploration for hydrocarbons and energy minerals.

AAPG Bulletin
www.aapg.org/bulletin/

A technical journal, recognized in the industry as the leading peer-reviewed publication for information on geoscience and the associated technology of the energy industry, that is received monthly in print or online by all members.

Online Publications – AAPG also publishes the complete *Bulletin* online for members and subscribers.

Online Bookstore – The AAPG Bookstore features all publications of AAPG as well as select publications from other earth science publishers and also is the point-of-sale for a new online Interactive Training modules.

American Biological Safety Association

Applied Biosafety: Journal of the American Biological Safety Association
www.absa.org/pubabj.html

A peer-review scientific journal committed to promoting global biosafety awareness and best practices to prevent occupational exposures and adverse environmental impacts related to biohazardous releases.

American Chemical Society

Journal of the American Chemical Society
http://pubs.acs.org/journal/jacsat

This journal is published weekly and is devoted to the publication of fundamental research papers in all areas of chemistry.

A full listing of the ACS publications can be found at http://pubs.acs.org/.

American Institute of Biological Sciences

BioScience
www.aibs.org/bioscience/

A peer-reviewed, heavily cited, monthly journal that presents readers with timely and authoritative overviews of current research in biology, accompanied by essays and discussion sections on education, public policy, history, and the conceptual underpinnings of the biological sciences.

American Society for Clinical Investigation

Journal of Clinical Investigation
www.jci.org/

A premier venue for critical advances in biomedical research, authoritative reviews, and commentaries that place research articles in context. The JCI currently publishes about 300 research articles annually.

American Society of Clinical Pathology

American Journal of Clinical Pathology
http://ajcp.ascpjournals.org/

A leading clinically oriented, peer-reviewed pathology and laboratory medicine research journal.

LABMEDICINE
http://labmed.ascpjournals.org/

A monthly periodical dedicated to providing the entire laboratory community with continuing education, career development and information about emerging technologies.

American Society of Human Genetics

The American Journal of Human Genetics
www.cell.com/AJHG/

A medical journal in the field of human genetics, this journal provides research and reviews relating to heredity in humans and to the application of genetic principles in medicine and public policy, as well as in related areas of molecular and cell biology.

Association of Women in Science

AWIS Magazine

A quarterly members-only publication, with professional articles on all topics pertaining to science, including scientific research findings, grant review panels, science and art, and the status of women in STEM.

AWIS In Action! Advocacy and Public Policy Newsletter

An Advocacy and Public Policy Newsletter, published monthly, gives the latest updates on legislative initiatives in Congress and nationwide news pertaining to women in STEM.

Biomedical Engineering Society

Annals of Biomedical Engineering
www.bmes.org/aws/BMES/pt/sp/pubs_annals

This journal is published monthly and presents original research in the following areas: tissue and cellular engineering and biotechnology; biomaterials and biological interfaces; biological signal processing and instrumentation; biomechanics, rheology, and molecular motion; dynamical, regulatory, and integrative biology; transport phenomena, systems analysis and electrophysiology; imaging.

Cellular and Molecular Bioengineering
http://associationdatabase.com/aws/BMES/pt/sp/pubs_bioengineering

This journal publishes original research that advances the study and control of mechanical, chemical, and electrical processes of the cell.

Cardiovascular Engineering & Technology (CVET)

A journal that publishes a spectrum of research in all aspects of cardiovascular physiology and medical treatment – from basic to translational research. It is the forum for academic and industrial investigators to disseminate research that utilizes engineering principles and methods to advance fundamental knowledge and technological solutions related to the cardiovascular system.

Biomedical Engineering NEWS
http://bmes.org/aws/BMES/pt/sp/bme_news_archive

BMES's monthly eBulletin.

Biophysical Society

Biophysical Journal
www.cell.com/biophysj/

Published semi-monthly, this journal publishes original articles, letters, and mini-reviews on biophysical topics in molecular, cellular and general biophysics.

Biophysical Society Newsletter

Published monthly, the newsletter provides members with the latest news in biophysics including upcoming events and programs run by the Society.

Botanical Society of America (BSA)

American Journal of Botany
www.botany.org/ajb/
www.amjbot.org/

A monthly peer-reviewed, scientific research journal focusing on developments and issues within the science of Botany.

Crop Science Society of America, American Society of Agronomy, and the Soil Science Society of America

Crop Science
www.crops.org/publications/cs

A publication that provides original research in crop breeding and genetics; crop physiology and metabolism; crop ecology, production, and management; seed physiology, production, and technology; turfgrass science; crop ecology, management, and quality; genomics, molecular genetics, and biotechnology; plant genetics resources; and pest management.

Journal of Plant Registrations
www.crops.org/publications/jpr

This journal publishes cultivar, germplasm, parental line, genetic stock, and mapping population registration manuscripts.

The Plant Genome
www.crops.org/publications/tpg

An open-access, electronic journal that provides readership with a short submission-to-online publication of the latest advances and breakthroughs in plant genomics research.

Journal of Environmental Quality
www.crops.org/publications/jeq

A journal published by ASA, CSSA, and SSSA. Papers are grouped by subject matter and cover water, soil, and atmospheric research as it relates to agriculture and the environment.

Journal of Natural Resources & Life Sciences Education
www.jnrlse.org/

A journal published by ASA along with nine cooperating societies (including CSSA and SSSA) that provides educators with latest teaching ideas in the life sciences, natural resources, and agriculture.

CSA News
www.crops.org/publications/csa-news

This monthly member magazine provides research and industry news for members of the American Society of Agronomy, Crop Science Society of America, and Soil Science Society of America.

The Societies publish a variety of scientific publications that are of interest to researchers in the agronomy, soil science, and crop science areas.

Agronomy Journal

A journal of agriculture and natural resource sciences. Articles convey original research in soil science, crop science, agroclimatology, agronomic modeling, production agriculture, instrumentation, and more.

Crops & Soils

A bimonthly magazine for the practicing professional in agronomy, crops, and soils.

Soil Science Society of America Journal

SSSA's publication that focuses on research relating to physics; chemistry; biology and biochemistry; fertility and plant nutrition; genesis, morphology, and classification; water management and conservation; forest, range, and wildland soils; nutrient management and soil and plant analysis; mineralogy; and wetland soils.

Vadose Zone Journal

An online publication issued four times a year in cooperation with the Geological Society of America that addresses the physical, chemical, and biological processes operating in the zone.

Soil Survey Horizons

This publication provides information relating to soil news, research updates, soil problems and solutions, history of soil survey, and personal essays from the lives of soil scientists in the field.

Federation of American Societies for Experimental Biology

The FASEB Journal
www.fasebj.org/

A monthly journal that publishes peer-reviewed, multidisciplinary original research articles, as well as editorials, reviews, and news of the life sciences, aimed at providing information not only to scientific organization but also to the general public. The Federation's goal is to inform more people about the issues and policies affecting the advancement of biological and biomedical sciences.

Genetics Society of America

GENETICS
www.genetics.org/

A monthly scientific journal publishing investigations bearing on heredity, genetics, biochemistry and molecular biology.

The GSA Reporter

The newsletter of The Genetics Society of America

G3: Genes, Genome, Genetics
www.g3journal.org/

G3 states on its website that it provides a forum for the publication of high-quality foundational research, particularly research that generates useful genetic and genomic information. It publishes research of interest to a wide range of biological disciplines, including microbiology, mycology, zoology, botany, and agriculture; research in established and emerging model organisms; and research in human and medical genetics.

Institute of Food Technologists (IFT)

Food Technology

A monthly food science and technology publication that addresses current issues related to food science and technology, including research, education, food engineering, food packaging, nutraceuticals, laboratory issues, and other items related to IFT.

Journal of Food Science

IFT's premier science journal that contains peer-reviewed reports of original research and critical reviews of all aspects of food science.

International Society for Pharmaceutical Engineers

Pharmaceutical Engineering
www.pharmaceuticalengineering.org/cs/publications_
section/pharmaceutical_engineering

A bi-monthly magazine for members-only whose feature articles provide practical application and specification information on the design, construction, supervision, and maintenance of process equipment, plant systems, instrumentation, and facilities.

Marine Technology Society

Marine Technology Society Journal
www.mtsociety.org/MTS_Journal_public/

A journal that provides the highest caliber, peer-reviewed papers on subjects of interest to the society which include marine technology, ocean science, marine policy and education. It is dedicated to publishing timely special issues on emerging ocean community concerns while also showcasing general interest and student-authored works.

Materials Research Society

Journal of Materials Research
www.mrs.org/jmr/

This journal is devoted to publishing new research that demonstrates a significant impact or advance of scientific understanding of interest to the materials research community.

Radiation Research Society

Radiation Research
www.rrjournal.org/

This journal publishes original and review articles dealing with radiation effects and related subjects in the areas of physics, chemistry, biology and medicine, including epidemiology and translational research.

rrsNEWS

A quarterly online newsletter of the Radiation Research Society.

Soil Society of America

Soil Science Society of America Journal

A peer-reviewed international journal published six times a year. Its contents focus on research relating to physics; chemistry; biology and biochemistry; fertility and plant nutrition; genesis, morphology, and classification; water management and conservation; forest, range, and wildland soils; nutrient management and soil and plant analysis; mineralogy; and wetland soils.

Society for Neuroscience

The Journal of Neuroscience
www.jneurosci.org/

Published weekly by the Society for Neuroscience, its mission is to publish:

- excellent, rigorously reviewed research in behavioral, systems and cognitive neuroscience
- cellular and molecular neuroscience
- development, plasticity, and repair neuroscience
- the neurobiology of disease

Neuroscience Quarterly

Neuroscience Quarterly is SfN's newsletter, published in winter, spring, summer and fall. NQ provides coverage of SfN news, efforts, events, and other issues important to the neuroscience community.

Neuroscience Nexus

The eNewsletter of the Society for Neuroscience.

Additional Resources:

Applied Clinical Trials
www.appliedclinicaltrialsonline.com/

A peer reviewed resource that provides a forum where pharmaceutical product developers can communicate with the medical researchers who test new products. Industry professionals learn effective and efficient solutions to challenges within the pharmaceutical environment.

American Pharmaceutical Review
www.americanpharmaceuticalreview.com

A bi-monthly publication of business and technology for the pharmaceutical industry, this journal provides information on the latest development and trends in areas such as drug delivery, information technology, research & development, analytical development and control, equipment and facility manufacturing and regulatory affairs.

In Silico Biology
www.bioinfo.de/isb

An international journal on computational molecular biology with focuses on the application of theoretical, mathematical, and computational tools in biological systems rather than to describe new algorithms. The basic idea is to promote the development of a more integrated view of living systems.

Bio-IT World
www.bio-itworld.com

A magazine that provides news, analysis, and opinion on enabling technologies that drive biomedical research and drug development, with emphasis on predictive biology, drug discovery, informatics, personalized medicine, and clinical trials. It focuses on the technologies deployed and strategic decisions made by companies in these areas, and their impact on performance.

The Journal of BioLaw & Business
www.biolawbusiness.com

An international journal published quarterly for biotechnology, pharmaceutical and management executives, attorneys, biomedical researchers, entrepreneurs, investors, risk managers, regulatory and policy analysts and other professionals interested in the biotechnology and life sciences sector.

Biomedical Market Group

www.Biomedical-market-news.com

Encompassing the *Biomedical Medical Group BMG/BMN, Biomedical Market Newsletter, Inc.* and *Medical E-Broadcasts™*, Biomedical Market Group is a leading medical industry information provider, publisher and news release distribution service.

Biomedical Market Group BMG|BMN is a medical industry information provider and publisher that serves the US medical community as well as medical organizations and medical symposia in Canada and the European Union.

Biomedical Market Newsletter, Inc. is the company's original news provider and newsletter. The Biomedical Market Newsletter assists medical industry organizations, conference organizers, and related companies in reaching out to medical industry professionals and related audiences.

Medical E-Broadcasts™ is the company's current core service and is a leading medical industry news release distribution service. It serves medical audiences worldwide and communicates news directly to medical industry professionals from both non-profits and corporate organizations.

BioPharm Solutions Suite

www.infinata.com/biopharma-solution.html

BioPharm Insight is a resource for proprietary forward-looking intelligence, market analytics and decision-making contacts that provides clients with an opportunity to develop competitive strategies and capitalize on ideal business developments.

BioPharm Clinical is source of global clinical data, investigator profiles and trial analytics that enables biopharma companies and CROs to assess study feasibility and optimize trial management.

BioPharm Devices is a guide to the medtech industry and includes detailed profiles on devices, companies, trials and contacts.

BioPharm Outsource is a database and online marketplace that connects biopharma companies with the product and service providers they need.

PSC Biotech

www.biotech.com

Incorporated in 1996, PSC Biotech Corporation is a global life sciences consultancy that provides validation and compliance consulting services and industry specific products to the pharmaceutical and biotech industries. They provide guidance and expertise in areas including quality systems, computer and equipment validation, automated process systems, commissioning and qualification of new and existing facilities, manufacturing and lab equipment systems.

BioTechniques
www.BioTechniques.com

An international journal that provides news features and peer-reviewed research on the latest in methods and techniques for lab scientists.

BioWire *Online*

www.sigmaaldrich.com

Published three times per year, this publication features innovative technologies from Sigma® Life Science.

Biomedical Research Alliance of New York

www.brany.com

Founded in 1998, the Biomedical Research Alliance of New York is a national organization that provides support services to sponsors and investigators involved in research in areas that include therapeutic, medical devices, biologic and diagnostic trials.

Brookhaven National Laboratory

www.bnl.gov

Established in 1947 on Long Island, New York, the Brookhaven National Laboratory is a multi-program national laboratory operated by the Brookhaven Science Associates for the US Department of Energy (DOE) and has received seven Nobel Prizes for discoveries made at the Lab. Its role for the DOE is to "produce excellent science and advanced technology with the cooperation, support, and appropriate involvement of our scientific and local communities." As stated on its website, it also strives to support the four DOE strategic missions:

- To conceive, design, construct, and operate complex, leading edge, user-oriented facilities in response to the needs of the DOE and the international community of users.
- To carry out basic and applied research in long-term, high-risk programs at the frontier of science.
- To develop advanced technologies that address national needs and to transfer them to other organizations and to the commercial sector.
- To disseminate technical knowledge, to educate new generations of scientists and engineers, to maintain technical capabilities in the nation's workforce, and to encourage scientific awareness in the general public.

Advanced Chemical Safety

www.chemical-safety.com

Advanced Chemical Safety is an international health, safety, and environmental protection consulting firm who assist their clients with the safe and effective handling of hazardous materials while remaining compliant with Federal, State and local Safety, Health and Environmental regulations.

IHS Chemical Week
www.chemweek.com

A leading source of news and analysis for key professionals concerned with the chemical, petrochemical, specialty chemicals and related industries and provides technical and business information to the chemical and process industries that use chemical to make everyday products.

Cold Spring Harbor Laboratory

www.cshl.edu/
www.dnalc.org/

Founded in 1890 as a biology teacher-training laboratory, the Cold Spring Harbor Laboratory (CSHL) is a private, not-for-profit research and education institution at the forefront of molecular biology and genetics.

One of its divisions, the DNA Learning Center (DNALC) is the world's first science center devoted entirely to genetics education. The Dolan DNALC, DNALC *West*, and *Harlem DNA Lab* extend the Laboratory's traditional research and postgraduate education mission to the college, precollege, and public levels. The Center states that its mission is "to prepare students and families to thrive in the gene age. We envision a day when all elementary students are exposed to principles of genetics and disease risk; when all high school students have the opportunity to do hands-on experiments with DNA; and when all families have access to genetic information they need to make informed health care choices."

In Focus

www.infocusmagazine.org

The National Academies magazine that features activities of the National Academies, which serves as independent advisers to the federal government on scientific and technical questions of national importance.

Lab Safety Institute

www.labsafety.org

Founded in 1978, the Lab Safety Institute (LSI) was founded to provide safety training for secondary school science teachers. The Institute has grown to become "An International Center for Health, Safety and Environmental Affairs" and is dedicated to providing the highest quality safety training, audits, inspections and consultation services in a variety of academic and non-academic environments.

LeadDiscovery

www.leaddiscovery.co.uk

In 1998 scientists founded LeadDiscovery to expedite drug discovery and pharmaceutical development. Their purpose is to help companies optimize drug discovery and product pipelines through the identification of breaking research and the in depth and expert evaluation of selected therapeutic areas.

They also seek to provide a platform for pharmaceutical, biotechnology and academic organizations wishing to increase the exposure of their research to the drug development community. They do this through their three key services: DailyUpdates, UpdatesPlus and PharmaReports.

LifeSciencesWorld

www.lifesciencesworld.com

LifeSciencesWorld.com is an online resource for biotechnology, pharmaceutical, medical devices and life sciences industries. It provides news, jobs, events, articles and a directory of organizations related to the life sciences field.

MolecularStation

www.molecularstation.com

Molecular Station is a molecular biology portal for research and science information that includes molecular
protocols and methods, listings for bioinformatic tools
and product information, the latest news and views on
research.

NatureJobs
www.nature.com/naturejobs/

Since 1999, this online science careers magazine has
featured science job vacancies and has guided scientists
along their career paths. It is a worldwide career resource for scientists, providing a wide range of career
advice and information to job seekers across Nature
Publishing Group journals as well as centrally at na-
turejobs.com.

Pharma Marketing Network

www.pharma-mkting.com

The Pharma Marketing Network seeks "to help pharmaceutical marketers advance their careers through
networking, sharing resources, and continuing professional education." Their newsletter, *Pharma Marketing
News*, was added to encourage discussion and promote
products and services of PHARMA-MKTING subscribers and advertisers.

Pharmaceutical Executive
www.pharmexec.com

A magazine that provides pharmaceutical industry news and analysis and is designed to meet the management and marketing needs of professionals in the pharmaceutical industry and provide information on marketing, sales, promotion, legal and regulatory issues.

PharmWeb

www.pharmweb.net

Launched in 1994, PharmWeb, the first pharmaceutical portal on the Internet, is an online community of pharmacy, pharmaceutical and healthcare-related professionals.

PipelineReview.com

www.pipelinereview.com

PipelineReview.com is the news center and online store of La Merie Business Intelligence and is focused on research and development in the biopharmaceutical industry.

Science*Daily*

www.sciencedaily.com

A news website that provides breaking news about latest scientific discoveries and features articles in many scientific fields including: astronomy, computer science, nanotechnology, medicine, psychology, sociology, anthropology, biology, geology, climate, space, physics, mathematics, chemistry, archeology, and paleontology.

PR Newswire

www.prnewswire.com

A global provider of multimedia platforms that enable marketers, corporate communicators, sustainability officers, public affairs and investor relations officers to leverage content to engage with their key audiences. They provide solutions to produce, optimize and target content – from rich media to online video to multimedia – and then distribute content and measure results across traditional, digital, mobile and social channels. Combining the world's largest multi-channel, multicultural content distribution and optimization network with comprehensive workflow tools and platforms, they enable the world's enterprises to engage opportunity everywhere it exists.

Coming Soon ...

About DataMotion Publishing

We Turn Experts into Authors

DataMotion Publishing was originally established to provide books, training materials and other published periodicals to Employment Practices Advisors, Inc., a human resources consulting firm.

Now a full service publishing business, DataMotion provides publishing and related support services to subject matter experts ranging from how-to guides, training materials and practitioners resources focusing on the human resources, legal and general business areas.

Services include:
- Manuscript Services
- Interior Book Design Services
- Cover Design
- Marketing and Promotion Services
- Book Website Development and SEO
- Registration Services

Our team of experts includes not only publishing and related professionals but also experienced writers and experts in the human resources, legal and business arenas.

www.datamotionpublishing.com
info@datamotionpublishing.com

www.ingramcontent.com/pod-product-compliance
Lightning Source LLC
Chambersburg PA
CBHW031924190326
41519CB00007B/401